Honing Your Knowledge

Honing Your Knowledge Skills

Mariana Funes and Nancy Johnson

OXFORD   AUCKLAND   BOSTON   JOHANNESBURG   MELBOURNE   NEW DELHI

Butterworth-Heinemann
Linacre House, Jordan Hill, Oxford OX2 8DP
225 Wildwood Avenue, Woburn, MA 01801-2041
A division of Reed Educational and Professional Publishing Ltd

A member of the Reed Elsevier plc group

First published 1998

British Library Cataloguing in Publication Data
Funes, Mariana
    Honing your knowledge skills – (New skills portfolio)
    1. Information resources management
    I. Title
    658.4'038

ISBN 0 7506 3699 8

Composition by Genesis Typesetting, Laser Quay, Rochester, Kent
Printed and bound in Great Britain

Learning is the process whereby knowledge is created through the transformation of experience.

(David Kolb)

Contents

Series editor's preface

The last decade has seen considerable change in the world of employment. Organizations have shed roles and management layers in their attempt to be more cost-effective, competitive and closer to their customers. The 'leaner organization' concept, with its emphasis on teamworking, better use of technologies and greater opportunities for innovation, certainly appears to be benefiting many organizations which have seen improvements in quality and the bottom line. The trend towards ongoing organizational change and restructuring appears set to continue.

What appears to be successful as an organizational strategy may offer fewer benefits to employees however. Changing work practices have carried in their wake a degree of confusion. Job security cannot be taken for granted and ongoing hard work seems the order of the day. The dividing line between work and other aspects of life becomes increasingly blurred as mobile phones, e-mail, the Internet, remote conferencing means that employees are expected to be accessible anywhere, anytime. Teleworking, hot-desking and project working means that employees are expected to be largely self-managing, flexible and adaptable, able to work in teams which cross organizational boundaries and are in some cases virtual.

A key development in recent times is the increasing call for employees to manage their own careers, to think of themselves as self-employed, to upgrade their skills at the same time as holding down demanding jobs. The old 'psychological contract' by which employees might expect continuous employment and prospects of promotion up a vertical hierarchy in return for loyalty and effective performance, seems to have been replaced by the notion that employees can gain long-term security only by developing their skills and making themselves employable. Of course in the world of organized employment, there has been a buyers' market for jobs except in certain fields such as IT where limited supplies of skilled employees mean that it is the employees who hold the whip hand.

I have been carrying out research into the changing workplace, in particular the effect of flatter organization structures on careers, since 1994. This is very much in line with the mission of Roffey Park Management Institute, where I work, to investigate issues relating to the health and well-being of people at work. I have found that many people find the challenges of coping with ongoing change and constant hard work debilitating. Other people seem to have found the recipe for success and energy in this changing context. I have studied what appears to make some people cope so much more effectively with change than others do, and I have looked at some of the skills used by these individuals. It is the range of skills which enables these employees not only to survive but thrive in constantly changing organizations which is the focus of this series.

This series is intended to provide a self-help skills development resource. The authors have been selected not just because of their undoubted expertise in the subject matter of their book, but also because they can write in a way which will enable you to develop or enhance your ability in the skill in question. This is not 'just a lot of theory'. Rather, each book offers a blend of practical activities, background information and examples from organizations and individuals, which should make sense whether you are simply dipping in for the odd idea, or working through in a systematic way. The books offer a range of insights and suggestions for further learning which will be useful to the serious self-developer. They focus on the truly transferable 'meta-skills' of lifelong learning.

So whether you are a specialist who recognizes the need to develop a broader business understanding, or a generalist who sees the need to develop some real 'knowledge' skills, this series has something to offer. Books in the series address some of the key skill areas for current and future success. Based on my research, I propose that the ability to think and act strategically is vital at any level in an organization. New approaches to thinking creatively and introducing innovation will become increasingly important, as will the ability to work in a range of different types of team. Project working is becoming commonplace and the 'new' project skills are as relevant to team members as to team leaders. As the workplace continues to evolve, the ability to work effectively in a range of networks and informal groupings will be valuable.

Above all, the people who acquire the ability to manage themselves and their time, including taking responsibility for their own career, are likely to be the people who can exercise genuine choice. Knowing what you want, developing your skills and having the ability to make things happen is likely to make you truly employable. As some organizations have already found to their cost, employees whose skills are in demand are able to make their own choices rather than having to rely on their employer. Perhaps making a commitment to yourself and your development is the surest guarantee of securing what is important to you. Good luck and enjoy the journey!

Linda Holbeche
Director of Research
Roffey Park Management Institute

Acknowledgements

We dedicate this book to all those who have participated in our knowledge conversations and thereby honed our own skills.

We would like to thank Brian Clegg for last-minute editing which allowed us to meet our deadlines.

Mariana Funes
Nancy Johnson

Introduction: a map for the journey

Knowledge Management is less about managing knowledge and more about managing people and change. (Don Tornberg, Vice-President of Progress, Amoco Corporation)

This book is a map for a journey, an essential journey for anyone working in the current frantic, confusing, fascinating world – the journey into knowledge.

The destination

You may have picked up this book to help you learn how to find out more information, gain more knowledge, more, more, more, more ... than others have. If you can acquire more knowledge more quickly, it just might give you a personal advantage and give your organization a competitive advantage.

Will any kind of knowledge do? If the business environment is changing so rapidly that we seem to be constantly chasing after new knowledge, what are the skills that we need in order to cope? These do not have to be about acquiring more of what is new, faster. This book is about how to work smartly, it is about understanding that management skills include effective knowledge working, and that it is useful to apply 'enough thinking' to the questions you ask. It is about deciding what is relevant once you begin to get some answers to your questions. We need to become expert knowledge managers to cope with a flood of information, to filter the useful and turn it to practical benefit. This means honing our analytic skills through understanding how to acquire knowledge *and* honing our intuitive skills through an understanding of skills of knowing.

Why travel at all?

Mary Catherine Bateson suggests that our culture places immense value on analysis. In her view our environment has changed so dramatically that 'analytical excellence is no longer sufficient on a stand-alone basis for processing information. The western success model needs a new component' (Bateson, 1997). This new component is intuition or tacit knowledge. The 'something more' that allows an expert to take the same information and analyses as everyone else and come up with a new and creative solution. It is only by integrating intuitive skills of knowing and analytic expertise that you can become an expert knowledge manager and cope with the new environment.

Let's remind ourselves of a few well-worn facts about changing work patterns and stress.

Organizations need employees who can adapt to a rapidly changing world. Organizational structures are changing. Ninety-five per cent of UK organizations either have delayered in the last few years or are considering it. The rigid, vertical structures of traditional organizations will not serve the needs of business in the next millennium. Flatter configurations are being introduced world-wide and in many different sectors. (Holbeche, 1994)

In the current climate our notion of career progression is also changing: 'to survive, individuals must be politically astute, build their own skills base and protect themselves from excessive work demands. No-one else is going to structure their career for them. It is a case of do-it-yourself.' In a recent newspaper article, Liz Mellon, an Assistant Professor at the London Business School, pointed out that stress, one of our biggest growth industries, costs about £7 billion in 40 million lost working days a year.

The idea of the do-it-yourself career is not new. The stress being caused by a trend towards taking individual responsibility for developing skills and careers is not new either. The lost working days and the millions of pounds increase year after year, and it may appear that one way out of the dilemma is to find faster ways in which we can process and acquire even more knowledge. But that is a mirage. The reason for making the journey is not to try to absorb everything but to acquire and understand the *right* knowledge for your requirements.

Mapping the map

We now map out the rest of the book, pulling together the main themes you will encounter.

The map

1. Why?

- A climate of change.
- Overcoming information overload.
- Experience and learning integrate to make knowledge.

2. Knowledge and experts

- What knowledge is
- Knowledge working.
- The knowledge management process.

3. Gathering data

- Extracting knowledge from an expert.
- Talking purposefully.
- Pitfalls.

4. Creating frameworks

- The skills of evaluating.
- Representing knowledge.
- Structures and processes.

5. Developing your intuition

- Why bother with skills of knowing?
- Understanding understanding.

6. Developing a know-how toolbag

- Understanding perception.
- Going beyond the words.
- Managing the mind.

7. The top ten tips

- Key points for moving from acquiring to understanding.
- Common pitfalls when thinking about knowledge.

8. Information technology

- Knowledge management.
- What technology can do for you.
- First steps.

9. Pulling it together

- Moving to a knowledge-driven organization
- Not *more* thinking but *enough* thinking.
- Knowledge, knowing and learning – a lifelong cycle.

1 Why become an expert knowledge manager?

Our objectives

- To set a context for our journey into knowledge skills.
- To present an overview of the key ideas to be explored.
- To start a self-awareness process: where are you now?

Where are we going?

As we have seen in the introductory chapter, the need for knowledge skills is driven by an increasing complexity in our working and living environment. To understand why these skills need to be developed, we will explore a little further the changes that make them necessary.

Organizational flux

The nature of careers and organizations is changing. Glynn (1996) points out that traditional organizations are low in tolerance for the diversity of people. They typically assume that business is rational, calculable and controllable. Their aim is to maximize profit and minimize costs. People are seen as a replaceable resource. De Geus shows that this approach is in conflict with the goal of becoming a long-lived organization.

Long-lived organizations need to be financially conservative, sensitive to the world outside, internally cohesive and highly tolerant of diversity. As organizations have less control over the external environment, they must change in response to that environment if they want to survive. This means that both individuals and organizations must meet certain conditions for learning: mobility, innovation and social propagation of innovations. For individuals to meet these conditions of learning, they need to be multiskilled, be able to adapt and be interpersonally sensitive.

One development that endangers these survival traits is the idea that knowledge is an entity that can exist independent of people. Knowledge management initiatives in large corporations have begun to talk of how to locate it, store it, transfer it and retrieve it.

A paradox

A quick review of the proceedings for a conference titled 'Practical Frameworks for effective knowledge management' (IIR Ltd, 1997) emphasizes the trend to attempt to separate knowledge and people. Yet such attempts to codify and set knowledge in concrete run totally counter to the needs of real organizations. This approach can discourage experts from contributing to expert systems, which is where the knowledge management revolution originates (Feigenbaum, McCorduck and Nii, 1988). It's hardly surprising, if the purpose of an expert system is to suck the expert dry and replace him or her with a computer, that there is resistance to implementing them. The fact is, the best expert systems support knowledge workers rather than replacing them, but this does not stop considerable harm from being done.

MORE INFO . . .

A brief history of knowledge management

Knowledge management is the process of representing part of one or more people's knowledge in a manner that allows it to be more effectively called on in the future. The approach emerged from work in artificial intelligence. In the 1950s we began to explore the possibilities that electronic computers could mimic human cognitive abilities: that they might be able to learn, to reason, to perceive, to understand language. A great deal of work followed in attempts to create the intelligent computer. One branch of this work produced expert systems, software for problem-solving that uses the knowledge of human experts who can solve tightly defined problems. Attempts to create an intelligent machine have given support to the assertion that knowledge, or intellectual capital, is key to organizational success.

In the artificial intelligence field, the knowledge is transferred from a human expert to a computer by specialists called knowledge engineers. They take the expert's experience and intuitions and develop computer software which 'contains' the expert's model of their area of expertise (or more frequently, a small segment of it).

Where is knowledge? Most of us have a fuzzy picture of something intangible 'inside people's heads'. Whether you intend to use that knowledge in a computer system or to build up your own expertise, the problems of getting your hands on it are much the same. Our work in this area spans over a decade of joint research and it has clearly taught us the problems that can arise when choosing an inappropriate metaphor to underpin any enterprise. In this case the danger is thinking of *knowledge as a resource*, a limited resource. This is such a commonly heard statement that it is easy to forget that it is actually a metaphor, not reality. Knowledge is not a resource. If it was, it could be extracted and utilized without the intervention of human beings. The reality is that the starting point for any project to acquire knowledge is the messy business of 'people's heads' and we must handle that messiness appropriately if we want clear observable results that show on the bottom line of our businesses.

We want this book to build a bridge from one body of knowledge to another, to ensure that the business community benefits from the experience of the expert systems community. We will, therefore, provide a practicable framework for knowledge management skills that is in line with a long-term strategy for business today, maximizing the likelihood of creating long-lived organizations.

WHY BECOME AN EXPERT KNOWLEDGE MANAGER?

MORE INFO . . .

Knowledge management initiatives

The real-life examples scattered through this chapter, compiled by Valerie Garrow, show a representative sample of knowledge management initiatives.

Using intelligence on competitors can be a prime candidate for knowledge management. Bulmers set up an information technology (IT) task force to study similar industries and supplied its engineers involved in bar-top maintenance/ installation with centrally served mobile computers to optimize itineraries. They found they could also use it to tip off salespeople on promotion opportunities.

Practical ways of managing information overload

Information overload is a fact of modern business life. We are flooded with information. The media, the post, e-mail, the Internet, business journals, business books – there is a never ending stream of inputs which it is impossible to ignore, but which could happily use up all your productive time if you gave them the chance.

Managers and professionals need to develop strategies to cope with information overload. They must stop gathering information just because it is available, and remember that learning creates knowledge and that we learn for a purpose. The urge to gather information can be driven by a number of requirements. It can be undertaken because you have been told to do it. It can be to escape doing 'real' work. It can be out of general interest in the world, or with a specific purpose and requirement in mind. Each is valid under the right circumstances. Most often, in business, the specific, focused approach is ideal, though a short burst of general interest browsing, for instance, is useful to spark new creative directions. The fact remains, though, that information overload must be coped with. Many of the skills that will be developed in this book are there to help you extract information that is relevant to the task in hand and integrate it into your personal knowledge.

1.1 The why of information

Think back over the last day. Which activities did you undertake that involved receiving information? Be quite broad about this –

include watching television, any conversations, reading etc. Jot down a specific note of each instance – not 'watched TV' but 'watched the six o'clock news'.

Draw up four columns, one for each of the reasons for gathering information above: 'Told to', 'Avoid real work', 'General curiosity', 'Specific task'. Put each example into one category. Try to be honest (especially with the second column) and do not allow yourself to be fuzzy – force each into the dominant column.

The purpose of this activity is to get a feel for your own approach to information. Bear it in mind as we look further into the nature of the expert knowledge manager. Be prepared to suppress your natural tendencies if you need to focus on a specific task. It is quite possible, but takes real determination.

You will find a similar message recurring throughout this book. We are all skilled knowledge managers, within our own personal way of doing things. To become experts, though, we need to be able to use a wider range of approaches, not just those that come naturally.

MORE INFO . . .

Knowledge management initiatives

Customer knowledge can be a major driver for knowledge initiatives. One organization has a Customer Knowledge Channel. Some organizations are trying 'Empathic Design', a technique for identifying unarticulated user needs. This might involve observing customers in the workplace, or an approach like the Microsoft 'wish line' where customers say what they would like the product to do.

Dealing with business problems

A problem exists only in relation to other people and other problems. Knowledge is used to change either the individual or the organization or both. Expert knowledge management is not about looking for absolute knowledge. This is a time-consuming and probably pointless enterprise, particularly in the messy contexts associated with employees and customers. Uncertainty and ambiguity are the order of the day in business.

Traditionally, organizations welcome rational and analytical approaches to knowledge management. Yet decision-makers are inundated with more information than they can handle with rational thinking alone; they are unable to turn information into knowledge. In order to do this we must integrate more-than-rationality into our approaches to handling information, and this is what we mean by becoming expert knowledge managers.

So, what is the best practice in organizations that are constantly changing, yet require the stability of effective performance? As a manager or professional in your organization, your ability to gather data accurately, put it together as useful information and transform this information into knowledge that the organization can benefit from is partly what your effectiveness is measured by. You meet your objectives when you have gone through a successful cycle of transforming meaningless data into knowledge that is of value to someone.

Becoming an expert knowledge manager means honing your knowledge skills. We are not necessarily talking of a single skill, as might be the case with honing your carpentry skills or your finance skills. Increasingly career paths are not linear. You may well need to think about building a portfolio of skills that can be applied in a number of contexts.

MORE INFO . . .

Becoming a chameleon

This lack of linearity need not be a bad thing. *The Chameleon Manager* by Brian Clegg (Butterworth-Heinemann, 1998) provides more information on developing the skills to work *your* way, building a personal portfolio whether you work for a single company or for many.

You need to find stability in a changing world. That internal stability can readily co-exist with external change if your focus is on developing yourself. Knowledge skills will easily fit in your portfolio and will be applicable to any number of areas. The expert systems community, unbeknown to itself, has done a lot of the hard work for you. Techniques and methods designed for the development of expert systems are intentionally independent of the subject they are used on, as they need to be applicable to a large number of areas of expertise. They are relevant whatever your particular knowledge needs.

Independence of subject

This independence of subject, called domain independence in expert systems circles, means that knowledge management techniques created for acquiring knowledge from experts are directly applicable to your organization. The expert knowledge you require will be particular to your organization, but it can be acquired using general skills. You are unlikely to use the knowledge you acquire to develop an expert computer system. Your purpose will more likely be about making explicit the intellectual resources of your organization and contributing to a common repository of knowledge.

With learning organizations being hailed as the way forward to the next millennium, we are setting out on a journey that will take us beyond the learning organization and into the knowledge organization. The way to go is not to depersonalize knowledge. Human beings have to apply knowledge to their experience and get results for it to be of use. David Kolb in his book on experiential learning puts it most clearly: 'It [knowledge] requires active learners to interact with, interpret and elaborate these symbols' (Kolb, 1985). You and the skills you possess are the intellectual assets of your organization.

This century is closing with the much heralded dawn of the knowledge era, but unless we can bring together the opposites of the industrial age, uniting what is human with what is technological, the term 'knowledge economy' may become an oxymoron. (Palmer, 1997)

Learning is creating knowledge

'Learning is the process whereby knowledge is created through the transformation of experience' (Kolb, 1995). Our day-to-day experience in the workplace provides the starting point for the acquisition of knowledge. We refer to this as data. Awareness of our biases in perceiving what is around us is key to our ability to create knowledge. The quality of the data we can acquire from the environment is dependent on our questioning skills (see Chapter 3) and the quality of our perception (see Chapter 6). It is impossible to be entirely objective. To develop effective knowledge skills we need to understand the biases we all impose on reality. In the next section we will explore a technique for understanding these biases.

Horner (1996) comments that 'modern psychology . . . is still based upon a representational theory of knowledge – that there is something in our heads which stands for the things in our world'. Nowhere is this more evident than in knowledge management. A fundamental requirement of knowledge management is that knowledge exists independent of any biological system and that it can be extracted from those who have it. Yet it is essential to include the knower in the system. Horner suggests that knowledge can simply be viewed as a change within the organism 'such that the organism fits better within its world'. In other words, knowledge is not an object, it is an adaptation to the environment. Kolb defines learning in the same way.

Knowledge as adaption

If knowledge is an adaption of a living being rather than a separable 'something', a machine, a computer application can only contain very static knowledge. In order for knowledge to be of use in real life and in real time it needs to be used by a person and constantly updated. Good knowledge must include people or the organization will soon have dead, irrelevant knowledge.

The skills of an expert knowledge manager

Throughout this book we will be exploring ways in which to integrate two forms of knowledge, analytic and tacit skills. It is in this integration that we can find ways to handle information overload and thus be able to work effectively with knowledge, as part of a knowledge management initiative or by ourselves.

Analytic knowledge is the familiar, easy to codify form. Tacit knowledge, on the other hand, is more holistic, less specific – it produces the intuitive leap. It is the integration of the two that defines an expert. Novices rely on explicit rule following (see Chapter 2), needing an analytical chain of steps to produce an outcome. Expertise goes beyond traditional logic to what Edward de Bono calls *water logic*. De Bono (1990) considers traditional logic (he refers to this as 'rock' logic) to be static and focused on what already is. Such logic, he suggests, is based on rigid categories, leading to argument and in-fighting rather than co-operation. By contrast he sees water logic representing the flow of the mind.

The mind is sometimes described as a self-patterning system. Imagine a solid plate of wax, across which a thin stream of hot liquid is poured. The liquid makes its own path, building a reusable pattern as it goes. This flexibility is the aim of water logic. Instead of asking what something is, water logic asks what something leads to. Coping with the fluid integration of analysis and intuition becomes an overarching goal for the manager of the future.

MORE INFO . . .

Knowledge management initiatives

American Airlines used its SABRE reservation system to achieve higher levels of capacity utilization than its competitors. This involved creating new knowledge as well as configuring existing knowledge.

The analytic skills are about gathering data, making sense of the data, and creating new knowledge; we explore these in the early chapters. The tacit skills are about developing your intuition. These skills of knowing are explored in Chapters 5 and 6.

Even after over thirty years of artificial intelligence research, machines have very limited perceptual abilities. By contrast, human beings can actually find a needle in a haystack or recognize their own car in a car park full of similar vehicles. It would be foolish to ignore this aspect of human capability, by allowing ourselves to be seduced by the dream of the knowledge-creation machine.

The organizations we work in today are more than moderately complex. We simplify them at our peril. Stored knowledge is only as useful as the people who use it, and to use it we must combine our skills of knowing with our analytic abilities, with a purpose in mind. Taking the machine metaphor and applying it to human endeavours too literally may never generate artificially intelligent machines but it could well generate naturally stupid humans. It would be very easy to simplify out of existence an essential survival trait: our adaptability.

1.2 The workman's tools

The old adage that it's a bad workman who blames his tools is an interesting one. It does not imply that there is anything wrong with having good tools, just that the difference between an expert and a poor worker is that the expert has such a good, flexible understanding of his or her area of knowledge that he or she can make do with inferior tools and still produce a masterpiece. The expert is, in de Bono's terms, applying water logic rather than rock logic.

Spend five minutes looking at an area you excel in. It does not matter what it is. Just jot down what the area is, and why you think you are different from a novice who has just been on a training course (and hence has all the theory, but none of the practice). If for some reason you had bad tools (or however these translate into your field of expertise), how would you manage, compared with the novice. Look out for water logic, combining tacit knowledge with analysis, in action.

Knowledge managers: where are you now?

Everyone filters reality through their own particular flavour of rose-tinted spectacles. When we process the data that is constantly flooding into us, there has to be some way of cutting down and organizing that data. But this process inevitably introduces bias. Before you can build on your knowledge skills, it is important to understand the way that you personally (and those around you) apply such filters and biases.

Just as a map of the physical world which was exactly the same scale as the world – so that a map a kilometre across was required to find your way across one kilometre of countryside – is impractical, so capturing all the knowledge we could acquire is impossible. The physical map uses contractions, symbols and abbreviations to compress as much information as is necessary into a small space. Similarly, we use knowledge maps, mental pictures that describe our areas of expertise, but do not cover every detail. We simplify to make the map useful, filtering out raw data in particular ways. For example:

- We choose to evaluate data with reference to our experience, the experience of others, and other data.
- We put knowledge into context by paying attention to timing: past, present or future.
- We selectively direct our attention away from the problem or towards the solution.
- Our knowledge can be organized into different sized chunks.
- We can choose to highlight many types of relationships in what we know, whether we are considering similarities or differences.
- Our knowledge can be structured as a set of options or procedures to follow.
- We can tie our knowledge more strongly to a particular sense – visual, auditory, touch etc. – in preference to others.

Human beings create internal knowledge maps of the world through their senses and filter information that comes in through them. We make sense of the world by deleting some of the data to which we could be paying attention. We create meaning by altering external data and changing it through our imagination; we distort what is around us. We create guides for action by selecting a limited number of examples and generalizing from them for future action. These three basic processes – deletion, distortion and generalization – are at the foundation of our perception and are what allows us to use language to create new bodies of knowledge for particular purposes.

1.3 Counting the minutes

In a formal meeting there is usually a point where the minutes of the last meeting are accepted as a true record. Yet, like your knowledge maps, the minutes of a meeting have passed through the three processes of deletion, distortion and generalization.

Spend a couple of minutes looking though the minutes of a meeting you have recently attended – preferably one you had a real interest in. Look out for these processes in action.

MORE INFO . . .

Knowledge management initiatives

AwiSE, a network of women in science, engineering and technology, provides external knowledge sharing – industry knowledge, benchmarking, best practice, professional networks across organizations. A similar effect can be seen when businesses use knowledge from different industries – for example, 3M used knowledge from prosthetic dentistry in matching skin colour for their hearing aids.

Five knowledge manager cameos

We have created the cameos below to highlight some of the ways knowledge maps can work. We will meet a group of typical (if caricatured) knowledge managers and imagine that we can read their thoughts . . .

Knowledge as black art: 'Ineffable-knowledge Kenny'

'How do they expect me to explain to them how to do a good job? It's all about years of experience and gut feel. I have substantial knowledge about spindlewicks, and how have I achieved it? How? Well, I tell you how. Experience and hard work. What I know is not something that can be made explicit, it is not something that I can let others have. The appropriate configuration of the product comes to me after I think long and hard about all the data that I have available to me and then I just know what the answer is. The answer presents itself to me almost by magic that the answer presents itself to me, and talking to other people about it just might make the magic go way. So give me the problem and I'll give you the solution. Don't ask me to teach others to do it; they just have to put in the time like I did. The important thing is to have an overall grasp of the problem. Use your feel for the situation to get a sense for what has to be done, that's all you ever need to do. You'll know, just trust yourself and all the many years and knowledge you have accumulated. This is something one just has, it can't be explained.'

How do you recognize Kenny?

He has created a myth around himself and what he knows. He believes that he is irreplaceable and that the only way others could learn is by putting in the years just as he has done. He does not believe that anybody can get at his knowledge, because having it and using it just happens through experience and not through conscious reflection. He is sometimes afraid of what could happen to him if his knowledge actually could be made explicit to be easily shared by others

Knowledge as truth: 'Evangelical Angelina'

'What a great course that was! I think everyone back at the ranch should learn this. It is *the* way for the future; we should let go of all other initiatives, old hat is what they are. This is different and new. Knowledge is constantly changing; there is so much to learn. I really believe that this time I've got it. Mind you, I thought the same thing a couple of months ago and then this new approach came. If only I could find a way to learn quicker and faster I would be able to know so much more and move forward in the company. I must let everyone know about this, though. I really believe that knowing this stuff will help everyone at work ... well not just at work, everyone everywhere! If they took this on, their problems would be a thing of the past. Oh God! There they are, all those books that I still haven't read. This weekend. Yes. I'll spend all weekend reading. I must get around to attending that speed reading course. I'll have so much more knowledge once I've done that. No time, there just is no time to find out more. For what purpose? I will find a purpose. The point is not to miss out.'

How do you recognize Evangelina?

Each time you meet her she is trying to convince you that the latest course or article or book that she read will hold the answer to all your problems. She is always telling how unique *this* particular approach is. She has forgotten that this one is just as unique and different as the one last month. She complains to you incessantly about how little time she has to find out and acquire more knowledge. The only way in which she can be effective is if she could find a way to keep up with all the new information she knows is available out there. She laughs as she tells you that she stayed up all night surfing the Net. There is just so much out there!

Knowledge as documentation: 'Procedural Tom'

'They need to learn the right way. I have the right procedure which I could teach them if only they listened. The important thing it to follow each step in order. "Oh no, we can't do that," they say. "Times are changing; you have to change with the times Tom." I keep asking my boss: "What are the steps? What do you want me to do differently?" Use your initiative; generate options. What does that mean? What are the steps I need to follow to generate these options? Nobody can tell me that. My knowledge has always had a clear structure and I am able to explain it to those new to the job. The problem is that they don't seem to want to do it the right way. It is no use to talk about the importance of "touchy feely" stuff, what matters is what can be specified in quantitative terms. That is what knowledge is. People just get in the way of following procedure; if only they were bothered to read the reports and manuals I write they would know how to do it right!'

How do you recognize Tom?

You will find Tom involved in quality control, documentation or technical areas. He might be promoted to Knowledge

Director. He believes that all knowledge can be boiled down to the right procedure and captured in Lotus Notes™. When the entire world is populated with machines which contain the captured knowledge it will all work like clockwork.

Knowledge as intuition: 'Right-brain rules Robert'

'We know so much more than we know we know! Our intuitive side gives our knowledge the common sense it needs to be of any use. There are so many connections to make in my job and outside it. We can learn from everything that happens to us. We can evolve our body of knowledge through understanding how to use all life experience to help us expand the knowledge we use in our job. The more we can perceive these links the more options we will have available to us. Generating options gives us choice and that is what we need for the organization of the future. I have a vision for management in the next millennium and it is about letting go of our compulsion to quantify and grabbing hold of our creativity. We must learn to trust our intuition and develop our emotional intelligence. All that cannot be put into equations and procedures. It is the only way in which we will be able to deal with the amount of information that we have to process as managers today.'

How do you recognize Robert?

Robert can often be found in personnel departments or consultancies, developing change programmes for the organization of the future. He complains that managers are stuck in their ways and about their negative attitudes and believes that they need to learn 'soft' skills. He wants his managers to trust their intuitive sides and cannot understand why *they* do not understand what he means. It seems obvious to him that analytical excellence is no longer enough. It is not sufficient on its own for information processing and effective decision-making. He can be found late at night pondering about what is wrong with his company that it cannot see the obvious . . . perhaps he should be looking to make a move.

Knowledge as relativity: 'Purposeful Paula'

'Sacred Cows. That is the problem. I used to have my own and now I'm absolutely sure that it is all relative. My sacred cow now and in the future is the relative and time-bounded nature of what we know. Our knowledge has a purpose: to move us towards a solution in a given context. Continuity and change are not opposing constructs. There is continuity in change and change in continuity. What guides us towards effective management of the future is an understanding of what is actually there and what we would like to have instead, we must understand knowledge in the context of our purpose. I know that what I know will map across different contexts, just like my ability to keep a home and children helps me parallel process the many tasks of my management career. The question is always, "what do I already know in another context that can help me here?" Thus saving time learning that which I can do without learning and maximizing the use of what I already know.'

How do you recognize Paula?

She may be a member of the board in your organization, a person who has reached the top in her career of choice. She is, above all, flexible. She can understand the uncertain nature of the future and can trust that the choices which she has made in the past will serve her in some way in the present. Knowledge is inextricably linked to who she is and what is important in her life, and it is also constantly being updated. She can understand the difference between acquiring knowledge as a commodity and knowledge as a dynamic process of knowing. On bad days she may wonder how on earth she manages so much ambiguity and longs for the days when she was still young enough to know it all!

Which filters are you already good at?

We have to filter information out to make our knowledge maps manageable, but we often use our preferences to justify not exploring beyond familiar territory. The key here is to become 'not you'. Your present filters provide your current knowledge skills, but as an expert knowledge manager your aim is to increase your ability. This process starts with awareness of where you are now. Here are some questions that might help you:

- Which of the cameos above came closest to representing your approach to knowledge management? Be honest, they are all valuable and all have their downsides too!
- What are the consequences, both those you want and those you don't want, of filtering life through each cameo? We

encourage you to come up with a list that has an equal number of wanted and unwanted consequences for each.

● How has your preferred self (in terms of the cameos above) helped you to get to the point of your career you are at right now?

Although we have personalized these distinct approaches to knowledge, in practice each cameo is one aspect of our personality that we may or may not be aware of consciously. The skill lies in recognizing and developing each of these aspects to respond to a greater variety of external demands. This flexibility will ensure that our knowledge maps are constantly evolving to meet organizational needs.

1.4 Cameo-spotting in your organization

Using the cameos that we have discussed and your findings from the reflection section, observe the filters that are in action around your organization:

○ *Are certain filters more valued organizationally than others?*

○ *How can you tell about other people's preferences?*

○ *Create a list of words you hear frequently in your workplace to help you sort out filters in use.*

○ *Construct new cameos to represent your findings. You are seeking answers to the question: 'how does my organization approach knowledge and its use?'*

MORE INFO . . .

Knowledge management initiatives

One approach is to use external sources (government, etc.) and companies offering information and communication technology. For example, companies like Electronic Data Systems Corporation (EDS), which demerged from GM Group and is now the world's largest IT services business, can provide information and communication technology.

1.5 Understanding your filters

We can now move on to a more detailed look at your own filters. It is popular to use self-assessment tools to increase your awareness and learn about what you may need to develop. This is a test with a difference. It will not ask you a huge number of questions, or need a complicated scoring procedure. It relies on your use of a tool you already excel at: language.

The profiling of your thinking processes is done through linguistic analysis. This is a lot easier than it sounds. All you need is some paper and a highlighter pen. By targeting the key words you prefer to use, you can identify the structure of your thinking process.

Step 1   *Write a short narrative (no more than one side of A4) in answer to the question: What is my approach to knowledge? Imagine you were talking to someone about your personal preferences. For example:*

'They need to learn the right way. I have the right procedure which I can teach them if only they listened. The important thing is to follow each step in order. Oh no, we can't do that, they say. Times are changing, you have to change with the times Tom. I keep asking my boss, what are the steps? What do you want me to do differently? What are the steps I need to follow to generate these options?'

Step 2   *Look at the list of filters below and highlight the key words in your narrative which fit with the filters. This will tell you about your current preferences. For example:*

'They need to learn the right way. I have the right procedure which I can teach them if only they listened. The important thing it to follow each step in order. Oh no, we can't do that, they say. Times are changing, you have to change with the times Tom. I keep asking my boss, what are the steps? What do you want

me to do differently? What are the steps I need to follow to generate these options?'

In this example Tom can be described as using a strong choice filter (must, need to, can't, have to) combined with a procedural reason filter (follow each step, the important thing, procedure, right way)

Step 3   *Consider how your narrative would change if you used different filters. You may like to rewrite the paragraphs a few more times using new filters, or just look at the options. This will help you become more flexible in what you attend to. In other words, to become 'not you'.*

Here is an example to get you started:

'They could learn a new way. I have a process which I can teach them if they want to listen. They could choose to follow the steps in the order which I have generated them. They could do that. Times are changing, you could choose to change with the times Tom. I keep asking my boss, what are some steps? What could I be doing differently? What are some steps I could follow to generate these options?'

In this new paragraph we have replaced the strong choice filter with a weak one, and the procedural reason filter with one where options rather than procedure provide the reasons. We have also changed at least one other filter – see if you can spot it. What changes in your experience as you read this new paragraph? Remember that we are talking about the same thing, all we have changed is how we use words to describe the experience.

Is this just playing with words? No, because the words we choose to use reflect how we filter and manage knowledge. We need to be aware of the consequences of our word choices; effective knowledge skills are about understanding that there is more to words than the subject matter they convey.

MORE INFO . . .

Flexible perception

The flexibility of your perception determines your ability to manage information and transform it into knowledge. We see this in more detail in Chapter 5. Using language in this flexible way can also pay huge dividends when you want to influence others. Read *Words that Change Minds* by Shelle Rose Chervet (1995) for an application of this tool to influencing others in business.

The perceptual filters list

Each of the filters listed below represents a different way of handling our perceptions. We have included a question to help define how the filter is used, and a set of variations within each filter. These variations are the ways in which we can sort or organize that category. The words listed after each distinction are sample words to target in the language you use. For example, the evidence filter has three variations: seeing, hearing and touching, which can be identified by targeting the particular type of sample words included under each. If a particular variant dominates your description, you have a preference for, say, visual information. At the same time you are likely to be reducing the impact of sound and touch information on your awareness.

It is important that you write your paragraph before familiarizing yourself with this list. People normally process these filters unconsciously and by making them explicit you will find yourself using them much more flexibly. In a sense you start becoming 'not you' as you become more aware of the distinctions you could make.

Evidence

QUESTION . . .

What sense do you prefer to use when knowledge processing?

- Seeing – see it in black and white, perspective, reflect, contrast.
- Hearing – hear, same wavelength, harmonic understanding.

- Touching – feel, grasp, get a sense for, a handle for the situation.

Decision factors

QUESTION . . .

How do you make decisions and implement changes in what you know?

- Comparison – more, better, same except, gradual improvement.
- Difference – new, totally different, completely changed, unique, revolutionary.
- Similarity – same as, in common with, as you always do, like before.

Attention

QUESTION . . .

Where is your attention when gathering information?

- Self – I, my decision, do it alone, total responsibility.
- Other – What do you think? How would you do it? Mary said it is best, you.
- Data – I carried out a survey, the statistics suggested, research is clear that.

Time frame

QUESTION . . .

What is your preference for attending to time?

- Past – use verbs in past tenses, I remember when, in my experience.
- Present – use verbs in present tense, now, right now.
- Future – future tenses, imagine, towards, expectations.

Choice

QUESTION . . .

Do you see things in black and white, or as possibilities?

- Strong – must, have to, ought to.
- Weak – could, may, an option would be.

Reason

QUESTION . . .

Do you justify your reason for action in terms of procedures or options?

- Procedural – speak in procedures, first, then, the right way, tried and tested.
- Options – break rules, opportunity, options, alternatives.

Direction

QUESTION . . .

What is the direction of your motivation to acquire knowledge?

- Towards goals – attain, gain, achieve, go, get, move forward.
- Away from problems – avoid, get away from, it's not bad enough yet, stop.

Chunk size

QUESTION . . .

How do you prefer to organize your knowledge?

- Specific – the details are, I have broken it down, minutiae, building blocks.
- Global – general perspective, the overall aim, broadly, bold brush strokes

The list is complete for our purposes, though there are many other categories in other applications of this framework (e.g. James and Woodsmall, 1988). Remember, though, that no filter is right or wrong; they are all useful in some context. We have not introduced you to this tool in order to help you put yourself and others in a box. This is always a danger with self-assessment. We want you to remember that just as you can choose the words you use so can you select the filters of your perception.

MORE INFO . . .

Knowledge management initiatives

Smart products are now being developed which contain knowledge inside them, e.g. tyres that warn motorists as they get low.

Summary

We have started our journey into honing your knowledge skills and set a context to help you understand why these skills are core to the manager of the next millennium. It is your ability to gather data accurately, put it together as useful information and transform it into the type of knowledge your organization can benefit from, that determines your effectiveness. You meet your objectives when you have gone through a successful cycle of transforming meaningless data into knowledge that is of value to someone.

Knowledge does not exist in isolation and people have to apply what they know to their experience and get results for any knowledge to be of use. You and the skills you possess are the intellectual capital of your organization.

A key concept we have introduced is that of expert knowledge managers, who can successfully integrate analytical and tacit skills. We have suggested that expertise is about using this combined logic, focused not on what is now, but on possible outcomes, when honing our knowledge skills.

What determines your ability to manage information and transform it into knowledge is the flexibility of your perception. The words we choose to use when describing our attitude to knowledge provide a good guide to our prefer-ences. We need to be aware of the consequences of these word choices, and to open up other possibilities by applying different filters to our perceptions.

Learning review

Some questions to help you review your learning from this chapter might be:

1 If you were to tell a colleague about this chapter what would you say?
2 What is the one nugget that you may find yourself quoting over coffee?
3 What did you disagree with, and what would be different in your knowledge map if you agreed with it instead?
4 What are five core characteristics of your approach to knowledge processing?
5 What, if any, are the gaps between your approach to knowledge and that of your organization?
6 What is one question you can formulate for yourself, which you now want answered having finished this chapter?

2 Knowledge and experts

Our objectives

- To understand more of what knowledge is.
- To enable you to understand the stages of development from novice to expert.
- To appreciate the complementary role of intuition and reason in your thinking.
- To give you tools for reflecting on your expertise.
- To explain the knowledge management process.

Just because we go about our daily lives using the knowledge we have according to need and immediate circumstance, it does not mean that we can manage knowledge professionally in this way. If we are going to create useful repositories of knowledge and develop the knowing skills, then we need to be disciplined about the way in which we maintain our knowledge. The next three chapters provide a broad range of techniques for handling knowledge in a systematic fashion so that you can enter it into your local knowledge management system under 'best practice' rather than a 'hunch that seemed to work at the time'!

2.1 Knowledge definition: part 1

Jot down on a piece of paper a one-line definition of knowledge. Do not agonize for ages, just write down your immediate thoughts.

That is the entire activity for now. We will come back to this later in the chapter. But do not go any further until you have done it. If you do not find it too painful, you could even scribble it in the margin of this book.

What is knowledge?

Knowledge is information that is relevant, actionable and likely to be partially tacit – not explicit or codified.
(Dorothy Leonard. Harvard Business School)

Knowledge could be defined as 'true justified belief'. This is distinguished from data (uninterpreted facts) and information (data put to use) by its inherent qualities of meaning and abstraction. Knowledge cannot be considered as being purely 'inside the head'. Instead, the essence of knowledge is embedded in social processes which can be shaped and enhanced so that individuals can grasp the essence through honed skills of knowing.

In our search for a knowledge sound bite we were struck by the fact that dictionary definitions have a characteristic flavour, emphasizing that an application is essential for knowledge to be considered worthwhile. To take a very simple example from everyday life, we value much less the successful pub quiz player who has acquired many facts than the wise builder whose barn remains standing through storm and tempest. The accumulation of knowledge as facts or truths does indeed impress us but knowledge of building and materials, put to use with skill built up over years, gains our admiration.

When you look up 'knowledge' in a dictionary you will see that the entry is far shorter than that for the action 'know'. The entry for knowledge says something like 'the fact or condition of knowing' (compact edition of the *Oxford English Dictionary*). It seems that by this definition, knowledge is the object of 'doing some knowing'. We would like you to breathe life into the basic idea, that 'doing the knowing' is the central feature of knowledge. That will take us away from concentrating too long on the storing and reorganizing of facts, data or information as a substitute for knowledge working. We hope that the idea 'knowledge = its representation' will then be suffocated.

Despite our unwillingness to give a definition we feel much like the blind man who could recognize an elephant from its parts. There are aspects of knowledge which need describing and we will do that immediately after some extra information on the nature of knowledge.

MORE INFO . . .

Knowledge

It is important to realize that you can think you know something, yet be wrong. If knowledge is 'true, justified belief', the truth and justification are not inside the head of the knower. The belief that the earth is flat is neither true nor justified. The phenomena by which we judge this are in the world: the earth really is curved. Knowledge stretches out beyond the knower and brings in the world. Many, including most information technologists, have adopted a position that knowledge is just a representation of the world, as though knowledge were a mental map by which we guide ourselves. Then knowledge management would be about storing and manipulating facts on paper or encoded in a powerful computer, with occasional forays into the world to apply the knowledge. While this view does have a hold on the IT knowledge management world, we must make it clear that we mean something different by knowledge.

While the truth of our beliefs is not something we decide, neither is it a matter of mapping reality. And the truth of our beliefs is tightly coupled to the justifications we have for holding them. This notion of justification is central. When knowers know something, they do so because they are held or declared to know according to standards of justification which lay outside their knowledge. The processes and standards by which this justification is achieved are grounded in social exchanges and embedded in social behaviour.

If we view knowledge as a social product this way, we can see why the notion of knowledge management makes sense. The essence of knowledge is embedded in social processes which can be enhanced so that individuals can get a better grasp of it.

KNOWLEDGE AND EXPERTS

So, and we cannot emphasize this enough, the way forward is through knowledge skills and their enhancement.
(Derived from Johnson, Johnson and Funes, 1998)

Knowing how and knowing that

This is the most basic distinction to bear in mind. It is the difference between being able to excise a brain tumour and being able to give a lecture on special techniques of brain surgery to colleagues. It is not a matter of the complexity of the tasks, for both involve esoteric knowledge. The operation requires a high level of expertise. The description of the operation involves more than a simple recipe of the task to be done. There is an awful lot of neurology to understand as well.

The distinction is not to be reduced to that between skills on the one hand and factual knowledge on the other, although these concepts do play a part. It is easy to lose your know-how through not practising your skills. For example, you might have become rusty at negotiating for resources but it would be relatively easy to update your knowledge of the current financial model of the company.

2.2 'How' and 'that' scores

Think back to the last weekend and note down ten different things you did. They can be anything at all – riding a bike, making a meal, reading a book. Against each give two scores out of ten reflecting your skill and your understanding.

When you have done this, look for significant variations. It is quite possible to be very good at something with very little understanding of it – you may be an excellent driver without the slightest ability to describe how a car works. Similarly you can be an armchair expert on music with no practical skill.

As a final part of the activity, think of a number of ways you might have to manage the knowledge you have. You might have to

*transfer it to someone else, or to make use of it in a different
context, or combine two bits of knowledge to come up with a third.
See if there is any relation between your scores and the ease with
which you can manage that knowledge. There is no right or wrong
answer, but the outcome is useful background when it comes to
improving your personal knowledge skills.*

Tacit and analytic knowledge

This distinction can sound rather similar to the previous one.
Tacit knowledge is knowledge that is inherently indescribable.
All those familiar things that we cannot explain in normal
words. Some examples are obvious: feeling grief, smelling a
favourite smell, having a hunch about something. While some
are better than others at using language and metaphor to put
across such ideas, the descriptions lack the explicitness of
analytic descriptions of other concepts. Contrast a description
of the new financial model with a description of that moment
when you knew you had succeeded in getting your budget
approved against all the odds.

Tacit knowledge cannot be made explicit using rules or
concept maps or other analytic descriptions. Unfortunately,
much that is interesting has this quality. Many skills exercised
by the expert plumber, martial arts expert or manager have an
indefinable quality which we recognize but which the expert
takes for granted. These great skills were traditionally passed
on to the next generation through some form of apprentice-
ship, usually involving much practice and learning from the
great and good, yet the skill or knowledge never appears in a
training manual. Tacit knowledge can seem like a holy grail,
always desired but never quite captured.

Expertise

Expertise is knowledge applied in context, the true Holy Grail
of the knowledge manager. There is no doubt that experts
know more than novices but it is the refining and polishing of
that knowledge through experience which turns them into
experts. They do not just amass more and more knowledge.
Their strength comes from knowing when to apply that
knowledge and, just as significantly, when not to act. They
know how to recover from mistakes without losing too much
ground. They know the shortcuts and when to invoke them.

Notice at this point we make no distinction between physical and intellectual tasks. Of course an expert jewellery maker and an expert negotiator are doing very different things, but their expertise can still be seen as using knowledge and skills in particular contexts: on this brooch or during this meeting. Each has lots of tacit knowledge largely to do with applying skills. Each has lots of explicit knowledge, about physical properties of metals or about group dynamics and finance. However, if you really want to know about jewellery-making or negotiation you have to try and capture the expertise. This means thinking in terms of the context in which the knowledge exists. To put it really simply, in order to acquire usable knowledge, you need to understand the range of tasks done by the expert involved and what part various bits of knowledge play during execution of the task. Activity 2.3, 'How much do I need to know to make that decision?', below gives you an opportunity to practise making relevant decisions.

2.3 How much do I need to know to make that decision?

The purpose of this exercise is to help you understand what kind of knowledge is needed to perform routine tasks in your company.

You have to plan for the impact of joining the European Monetary Union on your company, which supplies high-quality ceramics worldwide. Ideally you can ask your staff to brief you with a report:

- ○ *What are the issues?*
- ○ *What are our options?*
- ○ *What happens if we don't do anything?*

Then you can make a decision based on the predigested information. But even in this well-ordered world there will be a nagging doubt that some issue or detail which would have changed the picture might have been omitted. So you ask an assistant to give you some of the background knowledge which informed the report. You already know there are two trends that will directly influence your day-to-day trading:

    1 Interest rates will be lower and more stable.
    2 Transactions in foreign currency will be reduced.

You ask the assistant to list all the tasks in the company which will be directly affected by the two trends, then to list the facts needed task by task. Here is one we've started:

Task 5: Production of tap linings for domestic cold water supply

We need to know:

- Volume of business with EU and non-EU countries.
- Proportion and duration of staff effort spent on billing EU countries.
- Cost of currency transactions for that volume of business.
- Bank charges for servicing cash flow.

Task 5: Tap linings – domestic supply

Requirements:

find out volume	Ask about effort	Find out cost
EU and non-EU	Proportion and duration	Currency and general

Facts:

List of trading countries	Personnel involved	Accounts format
Number of models	Roles involved	Turnover
		Costing model

Clearly the activity is not complete with such a short list of tasks and facts to be ascertained and there will be much discussion on the 'facts'. But even with this simplistic table you can appreciate how much effort will be required to gather the information.

Now it's your turn. Spend five minutes constructing a table for another task on the list (Task 26):

Task 26: Maintaining catalogues of products

We need to know:
○
○
○

_____

Requirements:

Facts:

_____

In the real world, once you have a map of the dimensions of the problem, you can determine whether such factual information is actually available, can be coaxed out of the company database or needs to be created for your purpose. This will suggest a plan for finding out the facts and will involve you in finding out more about the work practices and procedures which make up your tasks.

Comment: *This is an exercise to get you into the mood for thinking 'task first – knowledge later'. The list of things to know or find out could be endless. Discipline your search by thinking about what level of explanation you need give at your proposal meeting. You need to have just a little bit more depth than you will present. This will save you from the deep embarrassment of revealing your limited understanding of economic and financial modelling in front of the accountants on the board.*

What is knowledge working?

Who are these knowledge workers? They are the familiar personnel, designers, consultants, analysts, facilitators and managers just as much as the 'chief knowledge officer' of management consultants Booze, Allen and Hamilton with super-librarians and researchers. And what do they do all day? They work at a knowledge level, applying knowledge to experience to make things happen – and along the way, acquiring more knowledge. Here we can highlight some of their more rarefied skills.

We agree with Nonaka (1991) that knowledge workers make tacit things more explicit. They may attempt to turn tacit knowledge into analytic explicit knowledge, but are doomed to fail in such alchemy. However, along the way, they can be instrumental in creating an enquiring and sharing culture in the organization. They can make some things more explicit by producing a rational representation of tasks and concepts, avoiding the tendency to rework problems already solved. They can capture some know-how, and describe it so that it can be disseminated more easily, preventing the worst excesses of corporate amnesia. They can make it practical to offload the dreary parts of making something happen to an automaton. In general knowledge workers can be most effective in teasing out what 3M calls the 'shadow organization'; all those assumptions and aspects of company culture which affect day-to-day productivity.

key concept

We characterize knowledge working as the application of what we currently know to our experience in order to generate more usable knowledge in a given context.

Becoming an expert

A clear and simple description of how we become experts is provided by Dreyfus and Dreyfus (1989). The following is a slightly simplified version.

The novice

The beginner learns to apply rules based on the obvious features of the situation. These rules are generally applied by rote. So a novice negotiator knows a lot of phrases with which to start a meeting, but may ignore subtle signals to get on with the meat of the discussion. He or she does not have the skill to move smoothly into the next stage. Without a good sense of the variety of attitudes and practices in meetings he or she acts without much reflection and if challenged will claim to be following a well-known rule of conversation. The novice correctly follows the rule, but does not understand the context in which that rule can be appropriately applied.

Advanced beginner

After lots of experience the novice learns when and when not to apply the rules. The advanced beginner develops an ear for situations indicating when they should curtail pleasantries or shut up completely. The advanced beginner uses more clues, and follows more complex rules. The advanced beginner learns from personal experience.

Competent performer

This is the stage where the complexity of the clues and the rules has overwhelmed performance: the negotiator has ended up speechless unable to choose between many communication techniques. Now the competent performer, for sake of sanity, must employ some organizing principle. Perhaps he or she defines a goal and proceeds accordingly. They may plan on the basis of a small set of salient factors. They may categorize the situation as one of several types with achievable outcomes. So our competent negotiator can prepare well, identifying a hierarchy of desirable outcomes. The competent performer recognizes the difference between ritual social behaviour and spontaneous, and can react appropriately. This is the level at which many of us stick.

Proficient performer

This is the level where intuition begins to come into play. The proficient know their task but may appear to have an idiosyncratic approach which works. It is suggested that the influence of experience is at its highest now. Recent events exert a strong pull. But he or she is still an avid rule-follower. So the proficient performer will consciously apply rules in an analytic way. Our negotiator will appear very skilled and will be proud of that skill.

Expert

As Dreyfus says, 'An expert generally knows what to do based on mature and practised understanding'. The expert appears not to deliberate over decisions, he or she simply makes them. The whole action appears fluent and coherent, unencumbered with plans or problem-solving. As with our natural skills of walking and talking we do not need to think about them in order to do them. In fact, reflecting on our expert performance tends to degrade it initially. But an expert does reflect critically on performance and intuitions. This is characteristic of experts. When something untoward happens they may react instinctively or may stop and think over a particularly important decision. It is easy to see this process in action with the skills of physical activity, reading and writing or musicianship. We tend to believe in the superior cognitive abilities of a mathematical genius. It is harder to recognize it in intellectual skills in the workplace. We often see the successful outcomes and may have an indefinable sense of having witnessed high levels of expertise, but the business expert does not seem to stand still long enough to be afforded full recognition.

What do the different stages of becoming an expert mean to you?

- In routine work you should be aware of the stage you and your team have attained so that you stretch in appropriate circumstances.
- You need to be aware of how to maintain your expertise.
- For career development, an audit of your level of expertise would help you target realistically.

2.4 Knowledge definition: part 2

Look back at your definition of knowledge in Activity 2.1. Could you reword it to fit what you now think?

Your concept of knowledge is liable to change as you work through this book. revisit this activity from time to time – see if your opinion is still the same.

The knowledge management process: a step-by-step guide

Knowledge management is now a productive business asset in its own right. Because it is seen as an asset, it has also been seen as a concern for senior management. Indeed, as a strategic asset, knowledge is a core management responsibility. In an increasingly complex, fluid world, it is pointless to rely on simple rules, re-creating past experience. There is a need for living knowledge, which takes in the current actions of competitors and partners. This enables managers to take intuitive leaps, based on experience but not constrained by it.

Knowledge management

We define knowledge management as the systematic and active development of ways to create, use, learn and share knowledge for a strategic purpose.

The knowledge management life cycle

Woodward (1988) characterizes knowledge engineering activity as having three phases. This cycle is adapted from general engineering design for the specialist design of software to support knowledge working. We can borrow and adapt it for our purposes, to gain clarity about what knowledge working should involve. In key words we could represent these phases as:

- requirements
- building
- use.

In the first phase the decisions are made about the scope of our knowledge requirements, for example choosing whether to look at the marketing of the new product or at ways of networking. Phase two is the detailed and iterative process of acquiring the knowledge, starting with identifying who holds the knowledge in the organization. This phase includes the design of any support systems required. In the third phase we go live by involving the relevant members of the organization.

Processes involved

It is helpful to look at the processes involved as part of a knowledge management exercise.

1 Identifying, consolidating and valuing knowledge as an intangible asset – mapping and building a knowledge repository/inventory. This is a phase one activity, setting up expectations and establishing needs and commitment to the initiative. Most knowledge management initiatives will suffer from the usual amount of scepticism. Perhaps most damaging will be the nagging doubt that this is a ploy to deskill or reduce the size of the workforce. The advent of expert systems, claiming to represent expertise, raises significant concern. Perhaps the antidote is to mention that software systems rarely put anyone out of a job but create many in the servicing of the resulting data processing activity in companies.

2 Acquiring and creating more knowledge, e.g. best practice and lessons learned. This is a phase two activity and is the most difficult. To perform it effectively, the knowledge worker needs to tap into the knowledge of experts. This is not trivial, but techniques have been developed to make it more practical; these are covered in Chapter 3.

3 Retaining, storing and classifying knowledge. This activity permeates the whole cycle, but is most intense in phase two. This is the activity which the knowledge management software vendors would have you believe constitutes the entirety of knowledge management.

4 Sharing and transferring knowledge, e.g. access from an Intranet or other collaborative technology. This occurs early in phase three of the cycle. If the approach taken in phase two was highly dependent on information technology, this activity will also tend to make heavy use of it. The sharing and transferring will be couched in terms like accessing and interacting with an electronic knowledge library.

5 Using and embodying knowledge in products/services, systems/processes. This, of course, is the whole point of the exercise; that the knowledge is reapplied in another context. It is unlikely the organization will arrive at this point without the support of information technology, but the instrument of change is not the technology itself. It is the point at which skills and expertise in knowledge management and the innovative ability of the individual come to the fore again.

2.5 Identifying a candidate knowledge management application

This exercise is an opportunity to practise the early stage of developing a knowledge management initiative.

Imagine that your company is to be split in two: a company that produces things and a consultancy firm. (In fact, consider the smallest unit of your company where this is practical to make the exercise speedy.) Your brief is to identify the company's knowledge assets. (In this fantasy land you may ignore the reality of financial imperatives!) But how to start? You have two types of resource:

- *statements about the company: financial and corporate*
- *the opinions of those who work in it.*

The temptation is to start by detailing the knowledge of handy experts, hoping that the accumulation of the descriptions of their expertise will give you a handle on the knowledge assets of the company. Save that for phase two.

First you should think hard about the 'knowers' in terms of their roles. A list of personnel grades or job descriptions will do as a starter set of categories of personnel. Resist the temptation to list what the individuals might know, instead concentrate on how they operate. For each category of personnel, list:

1. *How they come to learn their job – their knowing history.*
2. *How they make that job visible (by producing something, taking part in a team) – their knowledge outcome.*
3. *Whether transplanting this job holder to another industry would render them ineffective (no, for a logistics supervisor; yes, for an expert glass blower) – their knowledge skills.*

4   *Where do these workers obtain the seal of approval for their knowledge (the quality assurance process, their qualifications) – the knowledge standard for justification.*

5   *Classify your current understanding of each role as knowing how/knowing that and containing tacit/analytic knowledge – structuring the knowledge inventory.*

6   *Taking the stages of expertise outlined from novice to expert, try writing down the characteristics of at least one different stage for each job (in a real exercise you might do each stage for each job) – structuring the expertise inventory.*

our lists and notes and a dose of reflective thinking could well reveal some surprises about the knowledge assets in the company. For example, many an engineering company is also excellent at project management. You should now have enough information to make a plausible, if rather lightweight, argument for splitting the company on grounds of expertise.

Summary

- Knowledge is more than just a map of concepts.
- Useful concepts for characterizing knowledge are:
  - Knowing how versus knowing that.
  - Tacit versus analytic knowledge.
- Expertise is knowledge applied in context and this is the greatest asset.
- Knowledge working is the application of current knowledge to generate more knowledge in a given context.
- Expertise has several stages as characterized by Dreyfus and Dreyfus.
- The knowledge management process is made up of several subprocesses:
  - identifying, consolidating and valuing knowledge
  - building a knowledge repository
  - acquiring best practice
  - retaining, storing and classifying knowledge
  - sharing and transferring knowledge

- using and embodying knowledge of which the final stage depends on the finer skills of individual knowledge managers.

Learning review

Some questions to help you review your learning from this chapter might include:

1 What makes someone an expert?
2 How would you define knowledge if someone asked?
3 How would you distinguish between 'knowing how' and 'knowing that'?
4 Do you feel that tacit or explicit knowledge is most prevalent in your organization?
5 What is one question you can formulate for yourself, which you now want answered having finished this chapter?

3 Gathering data for effective knowledge working

Our objectives

- To introduce some simple techniques for obtaining knowledge from people.
- To enable you to select a range of structured, yet flexible approaches.

Systematic enquiry in the absence of real prior knowledge

Having explored the nature of knowledge, we must now turn to ways in which you can capture and preserve it. In this chapter we will concentrate on simple techniques for gathering knowledge from human sources. Many of the approaches in this chapter and the next will also serve you well when extracting knowledge from written sources, but the human source is the most difficult and the most rewarding.

We are going to assume that there is an area or topic of which you are largely ignorant and that you have a purpose for the knowledge you will acquire. This can be something very mundane: having to write a report on a division of the business of which you have no experience; investigating the feasibility of a new-fangled idea being applied in your company; picking up a new job quickly. These are all examples where your first inclination would be to ask someone to explain. When you are doing this you are exploiting your language ability in a conversational setting. You are already an expert at talking, so why do you need to self-consciously consider these well-honed skills? Because normal conversation is rarely knowledge-bearing in the explicit way you want it to be here. To get a better understanding of how conversation is used we need to explore some of its social aspects.

Conversations have structure and rules which we acknowledge unconsciously and invoke effortlessly. For example, there is the issue of turn-taking: we expect to do this and it has been shown that even infants can do it. You have seen the office bore ignoring turn-taking and knowingly exploiting the social convention that ending a conversation has to be by mutual consent, which he or she will not give. There are expectations about who should define the topic of conversation and who can change it, seen at its most explicit in that most stylized of conversational settings 'the meeting'.

These and many other well-learned conversational skills are already in your repertoire, but unreflective application could lead you into danger. If you set up your talk with your expert source as 'just a chat' and then take charge of turn-taking and the topic, you will find yourself conducting an interrogation with an increasingly mute source. If, intent on securing the knowledge, you do not allow for the normal niceties of human communication you will leave your source feeling used and exhausted.

So, assuming your major method of enquiry will be asking questions, what advice can we give?

Talking to people purposefully

There is a huge literature on interviewing subjects in experiments or surveys. Much of what concerns those researchers is the rigour and scientific integrity of the data they collect. Luckily we are spared such attention to procedure, for a little interviewer bias will do no real harm. But if you have any doubt about your impact as an interviewer, arrange to be videotaped in conversation. Nothing will give you so much insight into your personal foibles and characteristic body language. If you do not like what you see, then learn to adopt a less vivid persona – just for interviews.

This is not the place for all that sound, but third-hand advice, about the dos and don'ts of interviewing. But some awareness of the range of styles of interviewing available to you is helpful. An armchair activity follows.

3.1 Watch the interviewer

The television provides an ideal tutorial on interviewing skills. Look out for programmes with interviews. We suggest:

- *an extended political interview*
- *a chat show*
- *a police drama*
- *a children's programme with a 'phone-in'*
- *a counselling style interview where participants are revealing personal matters*
- *a live programme with short fact-finding interviews. e.g. news or consumer programmes.*

You should do your best to ignore the content of the interview and concentrate on the process and technique. For about ten minutes tally the types of questions asked as:

- *closed: with a yes/no answer*
- *open: with a more discursive answer.*

Then spend ten minutes watching how the interviewer, using language or other signals:

○   *encourages a response*
○   *reclaims control of the interview.*

If you tape the interview, watch the opening and closing sequence and see if you can spot the techniques used to move into and eventually out of the main body of the interview: notice when the real conversation starts and ends.

A real test of interviewer's skills is working with a child. It is well worth seeking out an opportunity to watch a child being interviewed. Children are particularly skilled at giving a line of response that they believe is being requested, so this is a good place to watch for interviewers giving clues unwittingly.

Having tried Activity 3.1 you will be ready to look at some of the component skills of interviewing. We will start by looking at the sort of questions you should use, but first there are two tips to bear in mind whenever interviewing:

● you should be very clear about the issues you wish to explore
● never forget that there are powerful social conventions operating, which you flout at your peril.

Identifying your questions

Blithely, we said that you should be very clear about the issues and questions you wish to explore. But, we hear you mutter, if I knew the issues I would already have the knowledge and would not need to ask. It is never that simple. All you will have at the beginning is an idea of the eventual destination for the knowledge you will seek. The easiest way to start is to list some of the issues you wish to explore, but express those issues in question format. Activity 3.2 is an example of starting with an initial list off the top of your head and then attempting to clarify your questions by considering the answers you expect.

3.2 Which questions do I ask?

Tony, sole proprietor of Tacky Toys Ltd. has called in Bill, the business process re-engineering (BPR) consultant to advise on future development. Bill must quickly demonstrate his ability to understand Tacky Toys. He knows he must provide a thorough analysis of the company with some recommendations that Tony has already thought of and a few surprises. So he wants answers to questions like:

- ○ *What is this business all about?*
- ○ *How many staff are involved in distribution?*
- ○ *What is this business for?*
- ○ *Who are its customers?*
- ○ *What are the forces for political or social reform which will influence the business?*
- ○ *Is there a cycle of activity in this business?*
- ○ *What local forces affect the annual cycle?*
- ○ *How can the employees work better?*
- ○ *. . . and so on.*

It will not have escaped your notice that this is an incomplete and thoroughly disorganized list. But Bill needs straight answers to all of these and more. Asking these questions directly will stimulate answers, but their usefulness (and straightness) will vary. If you doubt this, ask a few colleagues to try answering the first question about your own business without looking up the company mission statement. The answers will differ in tone, content and level of interpretation. So will it be with all questions that require anything other than a yes/no answer. Unlike many participants in normal conversation, you really are interested in the answers. You need to think about the kind of answer you will get even though you may have no idea of its content.

Take the questions above and categorize them by possible answer in the following ways:

- ○ *Those which ought to elicit a specific response which can be checked against some recorded data.*
- ○ *Those which you expect to be answered in abstract or general terms.*
- ○ *Those which you expect to elicit a description of an actual process.*
- ○ *Those which you expect to elicit a statement of values held by individuals.*

In your analysis it should soon become obvious that there is no one-to-one relationship between questions and answers. You could economize on effort by using one cleverly designed question to bring out several levels of answer, data, process and values for example.

To make the best of the interview you will need to develop the skill of handling the variety of answers without visibly losing the thread of the discussion. Here we have suggested that you start developing this skill through thinking about the range of answers you might get to an incomplete, naive list of questions. Then you can allow this exploratory process to guide you in sorting out a coherent list of initial questions.

You can continue to deepen this skill when we explore the skills of knowing in Chapter 6.

A coherent and complete set of questions

We cannot do this for you as the coherence will be specific to your area and heavily influenced by the purpose for your knowledge. However, we can offer some guidelines:

1 Pursue breadth first and then depth. Your initial questions will have to be rather general, but not vague. Questions on detail will follow naturally. Activity 3.2,

'Which questions do I ask?', was also an exercise aimed at reducing vagueness by the simple device of writing proper questions – with a capital letter at the beginning and a question mark at the end.

2 Record your talk and use a logbook. If for some reason recording is unacceptable, then share your logbook with your accomplice/informant. You will not be open to new topics or issues being suggested by your informant unless you reflect upon what has been communicated. It is surprising how often the informant makes quite strong suggestions of items of importance which the interviewer appears to ignore. Unless you listen to the talk or reflect long and hard on the notes taken you too will miss those ideas that would never have occurred to you.

MORE INFO . . .

A useful question structure (after Spradley, 1979)

James Spradley offers a comprehensive list of questions, and much advice, for anthropological research. The questions are useful as they are designed to elicit descriptions and explanations of customs practised in social groups. This is difficult for the informants: they know what goes on, but are unlikely to have ever tried to describe it. You are likely to hit very similar problems in any knowledge management project.

Spradley identifies three broad types:

- descriptive
- structural
- contrast.

Descriptive questions are easy to construct but not necessarily to answer, e.g. 'What do you do in the project review meeting?' However, in their simple interpretation you can elicit facts with these questions.

Structural questions are designed to obtain information about how your informant organizes the knowledge, e.g. 'What are the roles in project review meetings?' This may sound descriptive, but in the absence of a company document prescribing conduct in meetings, the reply will vary according to the perception of the participants.

Contrast questions can be used to gain explanation, e.g. 'What is the difference between Project Review Meetings and Project Appraisal Meetings?' Usually the answer will not be 'one word, actually'.

Refining your questions

Well-honed questions are the aim of this section. But all this ruminating on possible questions and likely answers seems to ignore our source, who will be providing the answers. The expert's response to your delicate phrasing should shape your next question. If you prepare a questionnaire with unvarying questions in a predetermined order you will feel safe but will be left with a bored informant who conveys little of the richness of his or her hard won experience and knowledge. The flexible approach of structuring the interview through well chosen but varied questions will be harder for you but more rewarding in the end. One way of doing this is to have alternative ways of asking the same question. Sometimes this is necessary when informants are baffled. Sometimes when the direction of the conversation wanders you will wish to focus on a half-finished discussion. Sometimes you will be checking your perception of a half-understood idea. In all these cases is worth having a few techniques for eliciting more on a topic.

First there are some communicative options:

- Echoing the last phrase uttered will usually act as a cue for the informant to keep talking.
- Requesting an illustration in the form of a diagram saves words.
- Asking for an example of a general or abstract point sometimes works too.
- Exploring the underlying metaphor is most successful. More of that in Chapters 5 and 6.

However, there is always room for asking the same question in another way.

activity

3.3 Asking the same question again

Imagine the dialogue:

'How does the changeover of shifts affect the production of the left flange on the primary rivet support?'

'Sorry don't get it!'

What do you say next? You have to find another way of asking the same general question (about work practices) here couched in a particular context.

Try writing three variants.

1 _____

2 _____

3 _____

Before reading our suggestions, go back and actually try the activity. Write three variants – it need not take more than a minute. Do not worry that you do not know what a primary rivet support is – be creative.

For the first, you could ask the same question by giving the context first and then the general question: 'When you are producing the left flange of the primary rivet support, how do you deal with the changeover of shifts?' Sometimes your colleague just needs a little more time to think.

For the second you could try another well understood context: 'Does the changeover to night shift affect the production of the variegated sprocket?' The second context acts as a cue for the original version.

For the third you could sway towards a very general question: 'How does the shift changeover affect production?' This could elicit an elegant and fluent response. If not, you still have the original version, now to be repeated but prefaced by: 'Let's look at a particular product that we talked about yesterday.'

This activity is excellent practice for honing your questioning skills. It helps you think hard about the purpose of your questions. It helps you think even harder than the previous activity about the kind of

*answers you are expecting. After you have absorbed Chapters 5
and 6 on skills of knowing you can revisit this activity with
increased imagination.*

The stages of purposeful talk

It will often be the case that the knowledge you require
cannot be gained in one conversation, that you foresee several
events where the knowledge emerges and matures over time.
This requires a process of extracting knowledge and analysing
the content of the talk. In this chapter we are concentrating
on the first part. In the next chapter we look at basic analysis
skills. As we aim to provide simple techniques at this point let
us look at the process in terms of the obvious stages:

- starting up.
- working up the knowledge.
- rounding down.

We assume throughout that you will be interviewing an
expert. You may choose to interpret this in a less precise way
than we stated in the previous chapter. Your 'expert' may be
just a colleague who knows something you wish to learn.

Starting up

The early stage of orientation requires attention. Even if you
are already acquainted with your expert you should prepare
the way for a change in relationship. This signal need be no
more than a phone call or visit to the place of work, even if it
is just the desk opposite, but should be clearly marked.

Homework

Prior to meeting your expert formally you ought to have an
opportunity to get to know some background. Typically this
will be some bedside reading, if it exists. Reading just a couple
of chapters of an elementary textbook will not come amiss.

Waste-a-body

The 'waste-a-body' technique is much practised by those who
have a friendly, local informant who is at least familiar with

the area. Having a local guide, a sort of subexpert, allows you to practise naive questions and correct your absurd pronunciation of special items of vocabulary. This is a technique much favoured by those planning to work with high-status experts, e.g. the Head of Planning and Production who might have little patience for explaining basic terms.

Beware the project presentation

There is no escaping the fact that the early orientation sessions are social events in so far as you are seeking access to the expert community, even if this is solely your colleague. The air may be heavy with social graces but many an enduring concept has been formed in the first meeting. You will certainly pick up much useful information very early on. If you are involved in a high-profile project you will have to be particularly vigilant. Experts playing a role in the presence of senior management can easily, and quite unintentionally, mislead you.

The first real session

During the first session after orientation, you hope to come away with a feel for the knowledge area and some of the key notions. It is probably unwise to begin with a very restricted form of interaction. Some of your initial set of questions and their variants will get you through the first hour or so. But there may be a case for starting with something a bit more structured. Helping the expert to prepare a four- or five-level hierarchy of key words is a good start. First ask your expert to list common terms, and then group and regroup them according to reasonable criteria of likeness, generality, or importance.

Case histories and examples

Some experts find it easier to recount tales of cases or case histories. You can ask for base, common, or unusual cases. The well rehearsed 'war story' is a rich source of those low frequency, but high calibre knowledge situations which only the truly wise can handle.

A collection of examples helps bring out the relative importance of one strategy or feature over another. Collect these opportunistically and analyse them later.

Task cycles

You will need an awareness of the sequence of events. So make a simple request for the cycle of activity in terms of characteristics (e.g. the length of a particular activity) and as much of the partial sequences as can be obtained. On a good or very long day, your informant expert may be able to describe separate tasks and their dependencies.

3.4 War stories

Think of a real example you have had of dealing with a difficult person. Write a single paragraph describing the specific experience, both the event and your feelings about it.

Now write a second paragraph, summarizing the experience in abstract terms. Describe dealing with someone of that kind in a general sense.

Look back over the two paragraphs. Note how much more effective the first paragraph, the war story, is at getting the message across. There is a danger in reading too much into a war story, as it is very specific and may not apply generally, but there is no doubt that this is a better way to get an understanding than through generalizations.

Working up the knowledge

Later on in the sessions, when lots of good information has emerged you can experiment with some of the indirect techniques. These are also useful if you have more than one informant in the room.

Indirect techniques

Ask the informants to role play a process with you or themselves. This is a real test of your grasp of the area, as two experts talking to each other quickly forget the presence of the neophyte.

Slightly easier to control is to ask the expert to instruct a novice in his or her black art. If prepared to risk your credibility you can ask your expert to take on the role of your teacher.

Setting problems

A very common approach to finding out what people know is by setting them problems and watching how they handle them. You can borrow the technique without its rigour (see 'More info' below) to great effect. Setting tasks or problems for your expert to solve can only be done when you believe you have a good grasp of the ideas. But it is also useful for checking your own perceptions. The time to choose this method is when you have begun to work with the expert on the principles or knowledge skills applied. There will come a time when you have produced a short list of general principles that you believe your expert brings to bear on all tasks or problems and you would like to sort out the details. Let us imagine working on the knowledge of an international marketing director. The task we are considering is prioritizing the activity for the month for the marketing teams.

During the course of the interviews the expert has mentioned the following as considerations when deciding how to allocate work to teams:

- volume of business which client brings
- amount of client contact last month
- volume of unfinished projects with the client
- urgency of next task to be done for the client, e.g. imminent lawsuit
- ease of communication – can you expect to get a response quickly
- current workload of the team.

You have no idea whether the expert has a favourite principle or how one gets selected in favour of another. So you make up a little scenario to obtain the choices, probably based on some real clients. You are likely to have more success with this indirect technique than asking the direct question: 'Under what conditions do you use strategy A, B and C?'

MORE INFO . . .

Giving people carefully crafted problems to solve as a means of investigating their thinking processes has a long, illustrious history in psychology research (see Newell and Simon [1972] for the classic statement of the timeless issues). The major difficulty with setting little puzzles and problems for your expert to solve is that the reasoning involved is not visible to you or to the expert. In fact the more complicated the problem, the more opaque is the process, with the expert uttering the odd word in between long thoughtful silences. This is not helpful for you as an enquirer. Usually the enquirer sets up the problem-solving session so that either the expert does the task and gives a running commentary or completes the task and is then debriefed.

When the expert talks during the activity it becomes obvious when he or she gets stuck, makes mistakes, backtracks, or has a leap forward so that you can 'see' how the problem-solving progresses. But having to talk at the same time as solving a complex problem does impede thinking. Some experts will begin by giving a commentary and then go silent when the interesting bit starts. If you interrupt, they lose their thread and then cannot solve the problem.

By talking afterwards, the expert can solve the problem and then generate some sort of description of what was going on during the problem solving. But the reconstruction after the fact will have serious omissions. Perhaps the blind alleys are not described and these are a useful source of information about conflicts and choices that are made along the way. As we saw in the last chapter, it is a habit of experts to deny they can explain how they arrived at a solution saying, 'I just knew it had to be like that'. You will still have the problem of uncovering explanations.

One way around the dilemma is to adopt a 'talk after' mode but videotape the expert solving the problem so that you can walk through the events again with questions like:

- What where you thinking then?
- Why did you pick up that piece of information at that point?

All of this may sound like game-playing but, in the hands of a competent interviewer, the indirect techniques can be very successful strategies for reviving flagging enthusiasm. Also it can be argued that such indirect techniques are the only sure route to global or meta-knowledge.

Observing

Observing your expert informants at work ought to be an easy way of finding out what is going on. However, we have left this to the end of the section as it is perhaps the most misleading approach to enquiry. Of course at some basic level watching an expert manipulate the tools of their trade is illuminating and it would be very odd not to see the expert in action. But unless you already know what is going on, you are not going to make much sense of the things you see. Again it is all a question of relevance. You only see what already makes sense to you.

In the case of purely intellectual expertise you will never 'see' the reasoning, only its result. This kind of knowledge is not available to observation. It may exist in conversations by e-mail or phone. It may involve several agents who do different things in different places. The chances of you being involved in a knowledge management project where the expertise is rarely visible is pretty high.

MORE INFO . . .

Participant observation

This method for gathering rich and meaningful information has been described by Patton as an 'omnibus field strategy' (Patton, 1990). Here the person doing the observation is part of the community being observed, and so plays a dual role. They are not detached observers as is required of scientific research and so accusations of lack of rigour can be brought. In knowledge einquiry, we want to avoid undue bias and so need to be somewhat detached, but we do not need to be 'an independent observer'. In truth such independence is impossible to attain by an insider employee and expensive when satisfied through calling in 'knowledge skills associates'.

The role of the participant observer is to 'simultaneously combine document analysis, interviewing of respondents and informants, direct participation and observation and introspection' (Denzin, 1978).

In participant observation the enquirer shares the life of the enquiree. In our terms this could be acting as an apprentice, learning on the job or shadowing. The challenge comes from retaining enough stamina and objectivity to reflect upon what is being observed.

The tools of the participant observer are field notes and informal interviews. The field notes, diary or logbook are the major source for reflection. Informal interviews form a large part of the information and are triggered by events in the daily life of the expert. The significance of these events, a conversation by the photocopier, a phone call, may not be immediately apparent to the inquirer browsing the expert's life. But as they are unrepeatable the participant observer must be always alert to the possibility of a knowledge-gathering interview.

Perhaps the most important aspect of participant observation is explaining the role to those you observe. Getting their permission to act in this rather socially intrusive way is essential.

Length of session

As your interview sessions with the expert become more focused there is far less recording and transcribing of discussions. On the whole, as you come to understand each other better, discussions will become more cryptic and transcripts less readable. Although more detail may be emerging, it is unlikely that the sessions will get longer. We recommend no more than half a day in dense conversation. Realistically, for most real-world business applications it is unlikely that sessions will last more than two hours.

Rounding down

The deadline looms and you must bring this enquiry to a close. The relationship with the expert informant is going well and if you have not done so already you should look to other, less expert players.

Enlarging the cast

Junior experts have not yet over-learned their jobs, and so will describe problems, strategies, and explanations long forgotten by mature experts. They can be a very fluent source of explanations when prompted to remember how they learned all this knowledge. Other experts off-site could be consulted. Good enquiry practice suggests testing the emergent knowledge with a wider population of experts or competent practitioners. Commercial considerations may mitigate against such openness, as will constraints on time and resources. If there is a client to receive the knowledge then now is the time to establish their needs in more detail. Now you will understand their concerns.

Using multiple sources

If you have the luxury of multiple sources you can use them to verify your knowledge. Revisit any books or reports on the subject. You should understand the theory better but find little overlap with other content. This should reassure you that you have gained much knowledge of a sort not already public. This is what you wanted. It is always possible that your lone informant was a great expert but a complete maverick. You can understand and preserve that knowledge but rendering it acceptable to a wider audience will need some thought.

There is also the problem of dealing with knowledge that has been 'created' during the purposeful talk. During debriefing, experts will occasionally say 'I knew that . . . but I never thought of it that way . . . now I will do things differently . . .', whereupon many a knowledge enquirer will panic, feeling that they are about to lose their own tenuous grip on the expert's knowledge. If this happens just wait, for the expert will begin to talk most fluently about the knowledge. You will be at the heart of the expertise.

In either of these situations there will be a lingering doubt about the idiosyncratic nature of the knowledge that you ought to check out. Structured interviews with other experts and stakeholders on specific aspects of the knowledge would yield grounds for believing whether the knowledge was indeed totally idiosyncratic. Using questionnaire format would be less time-consuming. Specific questions could be asked thus:

- In situation A, which of actions X, Y, or Z would you take next?
- How many of these criteria apply when taking a decision on . . . ?

Alternatively, the competent practitioner could be presented with descriptions of examples or problems collected earlier and asked to comment on the overlap with their own experience.

If you want to prepare a proposal for further resources you might collect some quantitative data to support your case of the form, e.g., 'When asked to state a preference, 2 out of 3 experts and 5 out of 10 competent practitioners prefer principle A'.

Getting the most from the lone expert

In the event of having limited access to only one expert you should still do something to check out your perceptions. For avid interviewers there are several types of questions which are effective in encouraging the expert to re-express the knowledge:

- You have told me about the order of events, now can you describe the causal relationships between those events? (This, of course, is not a question, it is a polite command.)
- When does X not happen?
- When does X not apply?
- Where is this viewpoint controversial?

These are all open-ended questions quite unlike many of the detail-seeking questions you will have been asking.

. . . and eventually

The rather innocent question 'How do you know when to stop?' is the most effective means of bringing the session to a close.

Pitfalls in gathering data

Getting it wrong by omitting the key concept

A project team of medics and technical people once set out to build a piece of computer software to diagnose and treat a life-threatening illness. Much time was spent on establishing the diagnostic and treatment process, the action of drugs, the dosage. Identifying the subtype of disease correctly was a crucial aspect.

In the initial trials of the prototype, the system did not diagnose like the experts. The team fiddled with the largely accurate detail for some time until someone suggested the problem was at the start of the process. They realized there was a suppressed distinction, known to all diagnosticians but not made explicit: that of diagnosable and non-diagnosable conditions. Some collections of symptoms are recognized early as not 'hanging together'. The system, correct in its detail, but lacking this high-level distinction repeatedly tried and failed to diagnose many cases. Not until the project manager realized that the team had missed the crucial organizing concept could he bring himself to jettison the first prototype and authorize a redesign of the system. This is clearly an example of how getting the knowledge wrong can catastrophically affect the production of a knowledge system.

Getting it wrong by not uncovering enough concepts

The business area was share dealing in one commodity. Knowledge engineers worked and worked, and eventually produced a system with two rules. The system was unacceptable to the traders who claimed 'it isn't that simple' and 'they didn't really get at our knowledge'.

Of course, the system was unacceptable so it was never put to test. The development team argued that demystifying the traders' knowledge might put their bonuses at risk but did not alter the fact that the knowledge they used was straightforward. They knew that the expertise did not lie with the obvious knowledge. The knowledge engineers believed that successful traders appeared to take more risks and make more deals, so profits could be highlighted and losses concealed in the noise of busy trading. The real knowledge lay outside of the easily expressed 'knowledge archive', a conceptual framework of decisions, categories and values.

As the system was unacceptable, the argument was never resolved. But it does indicate how the success of a knowledge management initiative is dependent on many more factors than the stuffing of knowledge terms into a document.

Summary

- Knowledge-bearing conversations are not just chats.
- Knowledge-bearing conversations are still conversations and subject to many of the normal social conventions.
- If you prepare your questions you will not be surprised by the answers.
- Use a variety of enquiry techniques.
- Fruitful observation relies on appreciating what is relevant
- The enquiry process starts general, becomes specific and then becomes general again.
- Involve other stakeholders later.

Learning review

Some questions to help you review your learning from this chapter might be:

1 What is the point of asking the same question in different ways?
2 What examples can you think of where a war story has been beneficial to understanding?
3 How could you prepare better for meetings with the purpose of gaining knowledge?
4 What can you learn from a professional interviewer?
5 If you had to describe the message of this chapter to a colleague, how would you put it across?

4 Creating frameworks when knowledge working

Our objectives

- To develop simple ideas for structuring knowledge.
- To experiment with some notations for preliminary analysis.
- To recognize stages in the analysis of early knowledge working.

Overview of the process for creating a framework

As we saw in the previous chapter, there are ways of managing the process of acquiring knowledge in a systematic and reflective way so that we are not overloaded by the sheer volume and complexity of it all. In this chapter we will explore some simple mechanisms to give structure to information, making it more practical to build it into your knowledge base. Let us take an analogy as the basis for this chapter. Imagine you are an avid collector of seventeenth-century silver, in particular, spoons. It would be important to you to be able to store your collection so that you could access a specific spoon easily. You would probably want to catalogue your treasures for insurance purposes. You would certainly want to enjoy the collection. In the most honest of all possible worlds you want the collection to be on show, or at least accessible with minimum effort.

Let us think now in terms of knowledge rather than spoons. Although acquiring knowledge is not merely about gathering and displaying esoteric things, there is a point to be made about how far we can consciously control the storage of our expensively acquired knowledge. Knowing that the human mind is theoretically capable of storing and processing more information than we need is not terribly informative: the display cabinet of your mind is certainly large enough! Looking at the research on memory is likewise a little disappointing for there is much to say about how well humans learn short strings of nonsense or simple sequences of events, and precious little on the mechanics of learning complex concepts from incomplete information. It is as if the display cabinet is large and probably safe but the doors are opaque and open only at predetermined times to allow access. And we have not even begun to consider all the intangibles of our expertise, our ability to classify a new object, to value it, to hide delight when securing a bargain and so on. This chapter is about developing simple ideas for structuring knowledge once we have begun to develop some conscious awareness of it. Chapter 5 will then go beyond these simple ideas and representations to consider strategies for improving *how* we structure.

To develop some familiarity with structuring tools and ideas let's stick with the collecting analogy. Having spent some time and effort acquiring this shiny new knowledge, you need to take steps to preserve it; to insure it against loss or damage. With a priceless artefact, you might reach for the camera or scanner or make a resin replica. Often you would not do much more than jot down the essential identifying marks. You would be making and storing some representation of the original so that, if lost, you could conjure up a reasonable description. A similar approach can be taken with knowledge. We rarely destroy or lose knowledge completely. It is more likely that we merely damage it by forgetting parts. This need to reconstruct dimly remembered ideas or skills is commonplace. You are trying to remember the rules of some long-forgotten childhood game to play with your 'I'm-bored-where's-the-remote-control children'. Or, if you were around the last time the company had a serious industrial relations problem, you could offer useful advice based on experience, if only you could remember the sequence of events and players clearly.

It is no good relying on the ineffable to get you through. All those ideas locked up in our heads which we say are too complicated to be explained are no use at all. Until the idea is made public in some way it cannot be recognized, transmitted, shared, refined or even destroyed. We are not suggesting that all ideas, knowledge and skills are meaningless unless made explicit. Nor are we denying that some perfectly ordinary ideas: the signals in my brain whilst typing this page; the skill of recognizing the smell of a rose, defy description. (Let us leave wine-tasting buffs out of it for a moment!) But our years as knowledge engineers have given us the confidence to claim that it is possible to elicit quite coherent descriptions from 'ineffable-knowledge Kenny' (Chapter 3). In short we have ways of making him talk, and even to agree that our diagrams are not too bad a description of some of his knowledge.

key concept

Representations

No genuine reflection will take place until you have a clear grasp of the nature of the object. So the first thing to do is to have a reliable and robust representation of the idea under scrutiny, in short, a good representation scheme.

The range of representation schemes

There are many ways to represent knowledge. Some are closely coupled with the technical tools used in developing software systems to store the knowledge. In fact sometimes the representation scheme looks suspiciously like a pidgin computer language. If you have already wrestled with the query language for your company database you will understand how difficult it can be to get meaningful information from the stored data. The data in the database has already been sanitized and structured in a coherent manner. It will be all the more difficult to handle the unfiltered and relatively unstructured data and knowledge you have assembled in your knowledge management project. And even if you do have an electronic company knowledge base awaiting your knowledge you are likely to be puzzled by the format you are supposed to use.

We are resisting the temptation to force the innocent to don the intellectual strait-jacket of communicating in computer-speak. There is more on the pearls and perils of using information technology to come in Chapter 8. For the moment we will concentrate on the early stages of organizing the knowledge into some structured form, perhaps to be tipped into a commonly held knowledge repository later. One of us was reminded of the advice of a very highly paid knowledge engineer who said: 'Save all the bits and pieces of knowledge and information. It will all be used somewhere in the system, for manuals and help . . . but only a tiny fraction will actually end up in the core programs . . .'

This seems to suggest that an attitude of acquisitiveness is useful. Collect all you can, at least initially. Expect to reclassify it for use later. Bear in mind that only a portion will survive for the formal report. But do not filter too early. We have already told you that one purpose of this book is to save you from the tyranny of having to cope with too much information and we still believe that. However, squidging information into manageable dumplings in a knowledge soup is what should concern us (Collins et al., 1985). The mere aggregation of knowledge is not the point. Finally, should you need any more convincing, think what happens when searching the Internet. So much to collect, so much to miss, so quick to drown in knowledge which *might* be important. You need to aggregate with a purpose in mind.

So what did this knowledge engineer use to identify and store potentially useful ideas? Some easy to learn schemes.

Prose

Never underestimate the power of prose. Writing a paragraph about something with full stops and capital letters allows you to use all the flexibility of ordinary language. At its best, prose harnesses our most powerful cognitive ability to convey the 'feel' of an idea. At its worst it provides a representation of the idea or skill which is cumbersome to absorb and too attenuated to remember. However, it is worth remarking that many an Arts graduate, including those from Harvard Business School, has spent years developing the skill of learning through analysing and producing prose or scripts. Many people out there are already well equipped.

Glossary

If a prose account strikes you as mere waffle, try writing a glossary item for each idea.

4.1 Writing glossary descriptions

Pick five items from your immediate vicinity, arranging them in alphabetical order. Write a three-sentence description of each beginning:

- ○ *An object with . . .*
- ○ *For . . .*
- ○ *Used by . . .*

and do not use a verb derived from the name of the object (e.g. an object for brushing).

Ask a wise nine-year-old to guess the identity of the object from the three sentence descriptions.

It is easy to be successful if you pick an obvious distinguishing feature for the object, e.g. an object with a big blue spot on the front or an object that does not have any legs, but of course many of your knowledge objects will be abstract – not so easy to describe in a sound bite. When doing this activity for real you will have to create more appropriate sound bites which pertain to the subject. The only way to decide what sort of description is appropriate is to experiment in this way and see how much your description expresses the salient features of the things you are describing.

Categories

Trying to classify ideas by placing them into invented or known categories is a common first step. The categories often start as a simple two- or three way distinction and can come from a previous life. You will probably already have a scheme you learned in management seminars, e.g. SWOT analysis (listing the strengths, weaknesses, opportunities and threats arising from different options). There are many category schemes from natural and biological science which allow categorization of a given artefact. Such schemes provide a set of terms to use as a skeleton structure so that you can begin to organize the concepts on a single sheet of paper.

It will not be long before you want to create your own categories based on the items you are trying to manage. One such scheme, *repertory grid analysis*, came from psychology and can be used as a method for generating appropriate categories. The activity which follows is based on repertory grid analysis and will give you a flavour of the approach. The result of applying the method, the categories produced, will be yours. We start by generating some two-way distinctions and investigate the links and overlaps.

4.2 Generating categories from raw data

Make a list of ten things you hate about meetings (force yourself to keep it down to ten).

Cut up the list into individual 'hates'. Pick any three at random. Stare at these three items and think about a feature which two share and the other does not, e.g. 'to do with personalities' versus 'to do with physical comfort', or 'easy to do' versus 'easy to learn'. Make a note of your distinction and return the three to the pile.

Pick again. Stare. Try to find a new distinction.

After several attempts look at the features and distinctions you generated. Does one seem to apply to more than the original threesome? Try fitting your ten items on to different features. It may be that your features need revising or tearing up. But the chances are you will generate a set of new categories that are appropriate for structuring this information.

This approach comes highly recommended when faced with a mound of information and a blank diskette called 'The Report'. It is a good way of getting started by generating some headings for the document. First list the points you know you wish to make (the items) and then generate some features. The features will suggest some headings for your report.

A pseudo-mathematical or scientific scheme

Here you might ask yourself fairly abstract questions:

- What are the elements, properties and relationships inherent in my knowledge?
- What is the topology of this chunk of knowledge?

These are hard questions to answer. So try something more straightforward:

- What is the shape?
- Which things are neighbours?
- Is there a common property or element – a sort of 'essence of points'?
- Is there a family resemblance between parts?
- Is there a sense of 'grain size' in that some parts are basic, some are subsumed in more complex parts, some others are superordinate parts?

The scheme in a textbook about the topic

Medical and other conditions can be described as symptoms, causes and aetiology. Almost anything can be thought of in terms of processes and entities. Another classic distinction is function, form and role. And no doubt the textbook will give a preprocessed scheme of type A,B,C.

If you write the ideas on cards, or Post-It notes you can experiment with categories by simply shifting the ideas around. Having generated some categories you can go on to develop a checklist or matrix of salient features, but the main aim is a classification system which will lead to a hierarchy of importance.

Structure: ways in which you can organize your emerging ideas

Hierarchy

This is a simple way of organizing your ideas which requires you to place some order of precedence on the items. For example to organize a hierarchy according to a principle of 'belongs to' is a nice easy way of sorting out detail from more general concerns. So in making an inventory of all our treasures we place the diamond brooch as belonging to 'jewellery' and the family Bible as 'books'. Not tremendously exciting a classification, but there is more. For we can experiment with other hierarchies and classification systems. Perhaps to create a hierarchy for 'value' including auction value, insurance value, sentimental value (see Figures 4.1 and 4.2). And another showing where the item is stored (in soup can, bank, on display but not in sight of window).

The physical activity of sorting and classifying, experimenting with higher-level ideas written on cards (in pencil if feeling indecisive) can help a great deal in the early stages of clarifying your thoughts. And, if we had not mentioned it early, you would have done it anyway, for it seems that those

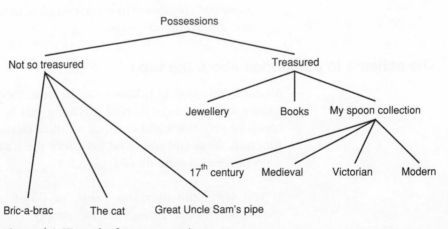

Figure 4.1 Hierarchy for my possessions

Figure 4.2
Hierarchy by value

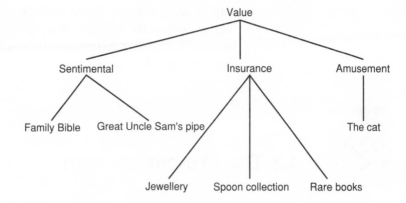

with a European-style education are keen on classification and category systems with a top to bottom look.

Mind maps or spider diagrams

A flexible form of hierarchy diagram is the mind map, a term coined by Tony Buzan (Buzan and Buzan, 1993). In the mind map, the key concept lies in the centre of the page, and the hierarchy works outwards in all directions, enabling different flavours of hierarchy to appear on the same diagram (see Figure 4.3). Because it can be built very flexibly, a good mind

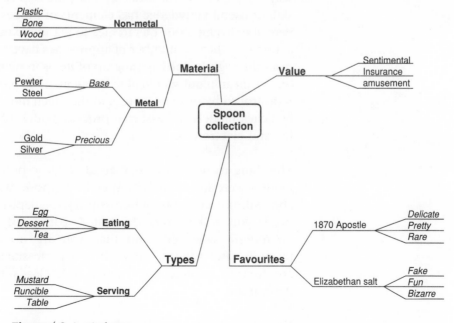

Figure 4.3 A mind map

map is an excellent mechanism for note-taking. Taken to a higher degree, by adding colour, images and more emphatic structure, a mind map can also be a vehicle for assessing and memorizing information.

4.3 The five-minute map

Take five minutes to draw a mind map of the business book you read most recently. Each major branch on the map could be a chapter of the book, or it could be a major concept. It is amazing how much of the valuable content of a full-length book can be fitted on a single page – and how much more memorable a good mind map is than the original book.

Processes: enlivening the structures

Treasured possessions can easily be classified in these simple ways, but most of our ideas are not pure objects. Almost any skill or useful knowledge has elements of process. We need a way of enlivening our hierarchies to get the extra richness of action into them. A number of approaches have been devised: from the slightly dotty joining up of items in hierarchies with bits of meaningful wool (blue = essential for process A, pink = destroyed by process B etc.), to the much more respectable feedback models and assorted process models of manufacturing and electronics.

The thing to remember is that all of these process-oriented models were invented for a specific purpose, which undeniably will not be yours. When you try to adapt them to your needs you will become frustrated, particularly with some *aficionado* who tells you that 'you are not using them properly'. But true to the spirit of a professional artist, you are free to explore the models if it leads to a decent description.

You can start simply with rules.

Rules

Generally rules are generated by thinking of events that occur and trying to break them down into simple statements like:

IF something happens THEN something else happens

This simple little phrase can be used to get the order of events straight in your mind. Unfortunately, life rarely falls into a neat sequence of discrete events, so you will generally need AND, BUT, OR, MAYBE and so on. When the number of linking words exceeds the number of happenings, perhaps it is time to stop.

A slight embellishment which helps the analysis stage is to drop the 'happens' from the rules and allow 'something' and 'something else' to be close relatives of items in your hierarchy. So from Figure 4.2, we might produce rules like

IF of sentimental value THEN security important.

IF security important THEN hide item.

or a little more sophisticatedly

IF of sentimental value THEN security important BUT consider enjoyment factor.

IF insurance value more important than amusement value THEN hide item.

might represent your attitude more realistically.

After experimenting with the pretend-it-is-English phrase IF . . . THEN . . . for a little time you will start to invent diagrams along these lines of that in Figure 4.4.

At this point it is best to resist the urge to use the paint and draw package on the laptop.

Figure 4.4
Boxes and arrows
diagrams

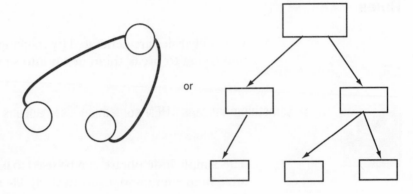

4.4 Rules rule

Consider a self-contained but not totally trivial activity or piece of knowledge; something like 'how to make a cup of coffee' or 'how to set a video recorder timer' (we did say not totally trivial).

Describe the knowledge in terms of rules (check the previous section for how these work).

When your description is complete, put it to one side for a few minutes. Then check back. What is missing? Have you taken into account the need to get everything to its starting conditions? For instance, if you were making coffee, is there anything saying 'IF all spoons dirty THEN wash one'?

Rules are a very valuable approach, but should be approached with caution because it is very easy to set up a structure which apparently represents the knowledge, but actually only covers a special case. Coming back after a few minutes (or next morning) will often help to jog the memory and to broaden the picture. This applies equally to representing your own knowledge or that of others. It is one of the reasons that it is generally better to have several short interviews than one long one (watch the police in action on a television cop show – you get the idea).

Status transition diagrams

There is a whole range of diagrams designed to represent the need for change. They generally look something like Figure 4.4, but are frequently embellished by the use of icons to show important features of the change. For our purposes we could work with a basic set:

- a sign meaning the idea, e.g.
- a sign meaning the connection with another idea, e.g. ▬▬▬▬
- a sign showing a start (s) and finish (f)
- a sign showing conditions which enable and disable the change ©

So, you can represent the notion of routine maintenance of an item in your collection as in Figure 4.5.

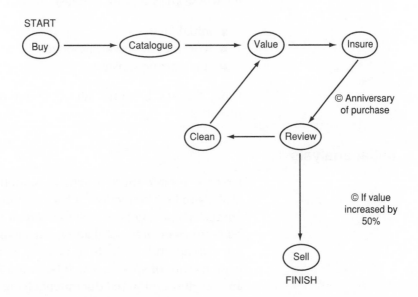

Figure 4.5
Simple diagram for
change management

Forming a view

By now you are well versed in generating representations of fragments of knowledge. You have the confidence to classify relatively simple facts and processes. It is a start but there are more difficult skills to learn. A key difficulty lies in the processes for managing emergent knowledge – how do you cope with the fact that your view of the knowledge will change as you become more sophisticated? This is usually called learning. Consider a scenario where you need to gather some esoteric knowledge within your company. Let us imagine this is a cutlery manufacturing company. All the spoon experts are about to take early retirement. The chairman knows that knowledge is a corporate resource and has given you six weeks to archive their knowledge. He has chosen you for your communication skills: the spoon section is notorious for creating a closed world with jargon and arcane practice. So, knowing not a lot about spoons, you are going to have to rely on your analytic and interpersonal skills. You are good at getting experts to talk about their knowledge and demonstrate their expertise (see Chapter 3) and armed with empty representation schemes and diagramming techniques (Chapter 4 so far), your major task is to recognize the significant elements lost in the background.

As with our look at conversation techniques, you could do a lot worse than to split the task into three stages:

- initial analysis
- working up the knowledge
- recognizing closure.

What follows is some advice about methods to help you progress.

Initial analysis

First we assume there is actually something to analyse. There is likely to be a collection of back editions of catalogues of the company's products as well as a few of your rivals'. There will be samples of successful and unsuccessful products and tools for making cutlery. If there is some guide to the design and manufacture of spoons it will be in the form of well-thumbed and illegibly annotated documents lying around the offices. In the absence of the definitive encyclopaedia of spoon production you have followed our advice in Chapter 3 and recorded an interview with the best expert asking him or her to describe the most important things a trainee should know about manufacturing spoons.

There are two desirable outcomes of the initial analysis; first, that you should be able to go to the next meeting with a 'sketch' of the whole area of expertise and, secondly, that you be able to ask sensible questions to obtain detail without irritating your source. Most start with the vocabulary of the experts and a classification of types. First make a copy of your transcript with plenty of room for scribbles. Read the transcript of your interview closely and try and identify spoon-maker's vocabulary. Make a glossary of the terms in the margin. Check your definitions against the index in books. For the obvious nouns and adjectives try constructing a hierarchy of types and subtypes, again in the margin.

Notice in Figure 4.6 how, at this early stage, a short phrase is used instead of a single word and that terms are repeated in

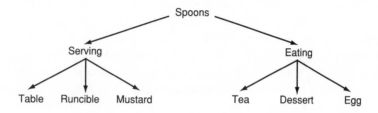

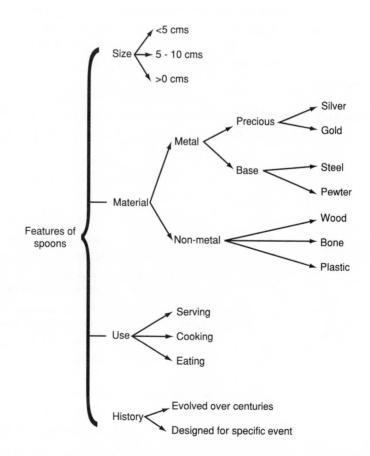

Figure 4.6
Margin sketches for spoons

different hierarchies. The 'features' fragment emphasizes descriptive categories which all spoons have. The notation with two forms of bracket is called a *systemic grammar network* and has proved effective for representing knowledge in linguistics, education and knowledge engineering. We include it here as a useful device for exploratory analysis.

MORE INFO . . .

Systemic grammar networks (SGN)

SGNs were invented by linguists to represent the functions of ordinary language. They show the relationships between items (called nodes). The relationship is expressed as a choice between alternatives. Either a mutually exclusive choice, denoted by a straight bracket, as between metals and non-metals in Figure 4.6. Or as a set of parallel distinctions, denoted by a curly bracket as in the size, material, use and history dimensions also of Figure 4.6. The names for the nodes come from the data under observation. By walking through the structure we can characterize items, e.g. This Orkney spoon has a size of less than 5 centimetres; is made of bone (a non-metal) and was used for eating, and its design is known to have evolved over centuries. Somewhere in my collection is a spoon between 5 and 10 centimetres long, made of base metal pewter, used as a serving spoon and designed for the coronation of Queen Charlotte. In fact all my spoons can be characterized by the full version of this network. The network represents a description of all actual spoons. To return to its roots; this is a grammar of spoons.

Creating such a structure is a good way of finding a way of describing the outline of a knowledge map. Note, however, that this structure does not express process well.

Where the expert is talking about process, experiment with fragmentary node and arrow diagrams (see Figure 4.5) to try and get a feel for the nature and sequence of events. Then take a step up and look again at your transcript to see if you have any indication of routine/base cases and the unusual/special purpose. At this stage, make a clean copy of your diagrams and notes to show your expert. Best to keep it fairly informal at this stage, showing signs of thought but not so well presented as to look flashy.

Now having become familiar with your expert's terms, turn to the written material. Your major problem will be to absorb more information into your fragmentary scheme and keep track of things which may not seem important yet. The problem of relevance stares us in the face. Of course this problem can be solved in the abstract by generating an index of all the material on your personal computer. But this does not actually solve the problem, as all you get is a huge amount of indexed material which is still too vast to absorb. The best you can do is segment and collate your information under the headings you have already identified in the talk with your expert. So first you separate the material into a few smaller heaps, in chronological order if there seems to be no obvious choice. Decide on a simple indexing scheme, documenting number, page, paragraph. Trawl the paperwork for items you recognize. Keep a note of what you recognize, where you recognized it and why you think there is an association. The latter is most important, as your idea of relevance will change. Duplicate your notes and do no more analysis until after the next meeting.

The final thing to do is to construct the agenda for the next meeting to include checking your perceptions of the sketch you made and asking for more detail in specific areas.

4.5 SGN writing

Systemic grammar networks are much easier to do than to describe. Look at the spoons example (Figure 4.6). Now try something similar for a subject that you know a lot about – it might be cars, or horses, or computers. Make sure that it is not process oriented. Try to put in some more of the curly brackets by introducing other groupings as well as features.

Working up the knowledge

The following cycles of talk, interpret and report back will be heavily influenced by the relationship you have with your sources. You will be checking that your understanding makes sense and filling in detail of your hierarchies and descriptions of the spoon expert's tasks. In addition you will be seeking ways of 'chunking' the knowledge. You can approach from several angles:

1 *Split the knowledge into 'core' and 'auxiliary'*. This is a crude distinction but checking your ideas with your expert is a good test of your grasp of the overall spoon manufacture task.

There will be other more subtle ways to modularize your knowledge. Most will be suggested by the nature of the task. Here we might use the obvious cycles of activity in any manufacturing process: identification of need, design, manufacture prototype, test etc. You may want to view the knowledge from different stakeholders' viewpoints: the needs of the production scheduler, suppliers, retailers.

Any such viewpoint will demand a new diagram using the same boxes and arrows but in different levels of detail and configuration. The final descriptions may be neither vital nor enduring but they will have helped you get around over and through your emergent knowledge.

2 *Seek gaps and inconsistencies as you see them*. There will be flaws in what you are told which need following up, but bear in mind that the characteristic secrecy of the spoon experts' serves a useful organizational purpose. It is there for their survival, and as such will be strongly protected. If you suggest that they are in error, you will hear the drawbridge be raised. Make sure that any error is attributed to your skills of listening rather than faults in the experts' knowledge.

Recognizing closure

At its most primitive this stage helps you decide when to stop. If you have a certain sort of mind, editing your diagrams and structures is at first fascinating, then compulsive. Eventually you will have to decide on the boundary of your knowledge. The symptoms are:

1 *Repetition of terms or processes*. This is easier to see when trawling documents but also happens with human experts. There is a sense of seeing or hearing the same thing.

2 *No more boxes.* You feel as though you have collected all the boxes and have at least a superficial knowledge of the contents of each.

3 *A usable map.* Your rough sketches have become a map for traversing the tasks of spoon manufacture.

Rarely, when already immersed in the compulsive stage, will you recognize that you have done enough. There is a hard test to decide whether your depth and breadth of knowledge is enough, that is, to go back to your original purpose or brief and write a series of questions to which your knowledge should be answers. The very general questions such as

What is it about a spoon that makes it versatile/popular/easy to make?

will give some feeling for the breadth of your knowledge. The more esoteric

What percentage of rhodium is acceptable in a European Union spoon?

will help plumb the depths.

A good rule of thumb is that your grasp extends slightly beyond the acceptable answers. Any further and you are in danger of regarding yourself as an expert and that will not do at all.

This sounds very long-winded. It need not be. The whole three-stage process could be run through in a couple of hours for a minor project – but it could take days if the need is to build knowledge in a key business area. This should not be too surprising – if it is so important to the business, it deserves more time.

What ways do you already use to develop structures?

The chances are you already have favourite ways of note-taking, summarizing and collating. To improve them you must become aware of them. So the first task is to monitor your habits.

One approach is to keep a logbook or journal of day-to-day events. This journal can accompany you everywhere, although make sure you explain that this is part of a self-improvement exercise, not a response to forgetfulness or incipient paranoia. Use it to note what happened and your reflections on the events. Collect your jottings for a month and then peruse them. Notice your favourite note-taking style and doodling characters. Ask yourself whether such notes and pictures would serve you well in recalling the event after six months. To get a grip on your practices, try asking a colleague whether the following are true or not:

- When I am trying to find out X, Y or Z I usually say, 'I was thinking about X in the shower this morning'.
- 'You always know I am puzzled when I . . . loosen my tie before 9.30/drink a lot of coffee/chat a lot.'

This exercise is not recommended for spouses or partners. It invariably elicits discomforting information and precipitates an ugly row.

Once you have an idea of your own habits it is time to use the journal to spot a few successful strategies in others.

If you find the idea of a journal too much trouble (which would be a shame – it can be very valuable), collect together the material where you typically make notes:

- a personal organizer
- Post-It notes on your desk
- a notebook
- loose sheets of paper.

Check out the styles that use with the same view to their effectiveness.

4.6 Generating categories from raw data

In the exercise on classifying your thoughts on hateful meetings (see Activity 4.2) you began to generate a series of distinctions (the features) which arose naturally from your own list. Now you need to do some work on refining those distinctions into an organized scheme for classification.

You can push the analysis a little by:

- ○ *looking for overlaps and repetition – e.g. when I classify things as 'to do with duration of meetings' I also classify them as 'to do with physical comfort'. So perhaps 'duration' is a subdistinction of 'comfort' for me (with a memo to yourself to schedule shorter meetings)*
- ○ *considering what features or items are missing from your original lists*
- ○ *considering just the distinctions in their own right and asking yourself questions like 'Is there a super distinction for any of my trios of elementary distinctions?'*

All of this can be done on your own until you emerge with a set of distinctions which seem to apply to many of your original concerns. But more insight or inspiration and certainly renewal of flagging enthusiasm comes from looking at someone else's effort. In this particular example it would be a mistake to try and produce a group set of distinctions. All the richness and beauty of your own ideas will be submerged in the inevitable blandness of the result. But there are plenty of areas where shared knowledge needs to be made explicit, e.g. where the work practices are nowhere codified, different people work with different parts and someone has the job of getting a grip on the whole task.

A good example for practice is handling customer complaints in your company, and a group exercise follows.

4.7 Handling customer complaints (group exercise)

Form several teams, asking the disparate workers to generate a group description of the task through a pyramid activity. Each worker starts the process by working on their own for twenty minutes generating a description of their role, e.g. as telephone contact, signer of cheques for refunds. Prompting them to use a common set of diagramming techniques will save time and effort now and later.

Then, working in a pair with another of the same role, they make a joint description. Similarly two pairs join to make a four-strong description. Even eights can work. When an explicit description of each role is forthcoming it may be appropriate to re-form the original teams and start work on the several team pictures of the whole task, knowing there is an agreed and well understood description of each role in use in each team.

Summary

This chapter is about developing simple ideas for structuring knowledge once we have begun to develop some conscious awareness of it.

- You must make the knowledge explicit in an expressive representation.
- In the early stages of analysing your embryonic knowledge, simple pencil and paper techniques are useful.
- The art of generating descriptive categories is a skill to develop.
- Representing process will also be your concern.
- You can grow your knowledge structures through the stages of initial analysis, working up the knowledge and recognizing closure.

Learning review

Some questions to help you review your learning from this chapter might be:

1 What is the purpose of a framework?
2 Which types of diagram seem most useful to you? Why?
3 What knowledge frameworks do you see in use in your workplace?
4 Are there types of knowledge which don't fit frameworks well?
5 What is one question you can formulate for yourself, which you now want answered having finished this chapter?

5 Skills of knowing

 Serendipity: a word invented by Horace Walpole (1717–1797) in a 1754 letter in which Walpole told about the 3 princes of Serendip, 'who were always making discoveries, by accident and sagacity of things they were not in quest of.' (quoted in Shapiro, 1995)

Our objectives

- To help you understand the know-how needed to manage knowledge further.
- To reflect on the skills that support the techniques of previous chapters.
- To help you become aware of the ways you make sense of you environment in order to manage knowledge.
- To help you understand the underlying foundations of knowledge work.

When we started this journey we talked about the integration of analytical and tacit skills as key to the manager of the future. We defined expert knowledge managers as those who had achieved this balance between the tacit and the analytical aspects of themselves. The techniques we have explored in the previous chapter will have helped your analytical skills; this chapter explores the tacit skills that support these techniques. We have explored the basics and we now move into the foundation aspects of knowledge work.

The key distinction we are making is that we are shifting our attention from being outward-looking to being inward-looking. We have practised technique. Successful knowledge work requires that the techniques be supported with well-honed skills of knowing. So, we are now changing gear to work on the theoretical and reflective aspects of knowledge work. You need this understanding to become an expert knowledge manager; we will look in more depth at the reasons for exploring these aspects of knowledge work.

Why bother with skills of knowing?

Skills of knowing are less visible and tangible than the analytical skills we have explored so far. Cognitive processes are difficult to study because 'there is no camera that takes pictures of a [manager's] thoughts' (Wofford, 1994). There is, however, a lot of useful information that can be made explicit and is of practical use to the expert knowledge manager. This chapter is about the process we go through in our mind to analyse and create knowledge. We typically reuse patterns that hold true in physical reality to organize abstract knowledge in our minds. The way real things behave becomes a metaphor to cope with abstracts. When we gain an understanding of something, we are normally building a metaphor that parallels its structure. This notion creates fundamental difficulties for the creation of flexible computer systems but is good news for you as an expert knowledge manager.

For the purposes of this chapter we are asking that you shift your attention from an external focus to an internal one. We want to explore our ability to understand the world, an amazing process that enables us to make sense of what could be a plethora of stimuli without pattern. To learn the knowledge skills we have explored so far, you have performed remarkable feats of cognition. The next activity will show you what we mean.

5.1 Remarkable feats of cognition

(adapted from Johnson, 1987)

Step 1   *Find a comfortable position, either sitting or lying down. It will probably help to close your eyes (though that makes reading these instructions harder).*

Step 2   *Consider for a moment what it is like to be your body in space. The many orientational feats you perform as you go through your daily activities. The many movements that may occur in the first few minutes of an ordinary day.*

Step 3   *You wake up from sleeping and peer out from the covers into your room, you come out of your sleepy state and pull yourself out of the bed, climb into your dressing-gown, have a good stretch, walk in a daze out of your room and into the bathroom, you look in the mirror and see your face staring out at you . . .*

Step 4   *Now turn your attention to your body. Notice that there is a clear boundary between what you perceive as being in your body and outside of it. Trace that boundary around your body. Your body is in the room and the room may contain other bodies.*

Step 5   *Open your eyes. Look around you. Now fix your eyes on one point in the room. Notice that some things are in your visual field and others are only just out of it. The centre of your visual field is clear, while the periphery is fuzzy.*

Step 6   *Now start gently moving your body and notice that it has many parts: your feet, your hands, your arms, and so on . . . many parts that form the whole of you. What is that like? Part of a whole?*

Step 7   *Find a sympathetic ear and spend five minutes describing what you have experienced.*

This activity is helping you attend to only a tiny aspect of what it means to make sense of your world, i.e. the way in which you orient yourself in space. The building blocks of understanding are many. If you are interested in this area we explore this topic in detail below.

MORE INFO . . .

Embodied image schemata

There are number of basic components to our ability to understand our world. Cognitive semanticist George Lakoff (1987) refers to these as embodied image schemata, where he looks at the particular aspects of the body which we use as a metaphor to get a hold on tacit knowledge (note, by the way that 'get a hold on' is

SKILLS OF KNOWING

itself making metaphorical use of a physical action of the body to describe an abstract concept). Take, for example, the source-path-goal schema:

- *Bodily experience.* When we move anywhere there is a place we start from, a place we end up at, a sequence of contiguous locations which connect the starting point with the end point and a direction we follow.
- *Structural elements.* A source, a destination, a path and a direction to the destination.
- *Basic logic.* From a source to a destination I must pass through intermediate points on a path and the further along the path I am the more time has passed.
- *Sample metaphor.* We can think of purposes as destinations. So, I have gone a long way in achieving my purpose, he got side-tracked from his purpose, this is getting in the way of my purpose.

Jack Heggie (1994) has provided more examples of the mind-is-body metaphor, and describes how these metaphors structure experience. He calls them 'body-mind' phrases. His examples include: 'get your head straight', 'you are unbalanced', 'being bent out of shape', 'you are really together', 'I behaved in a spineless manner', 'she made me feel an inch tall', 'I have finally come to my senses', 'she has her feet firmly on the ground'.

When we understand something we have used this process to provide structure to our virtual world of mind.

We take our cognitive abilities for granted and do not come into the world equipped with a maintenance manual. In honing our knowledge management skills, we need to bring our skills of knowing into conscious awareness, give them a good clean and learn how to optimize *how* we do what we do.

So why bother with all this self-awareness and internal focus? After all, is it not the case that we use these skills of knowing already without needing to direct our conscious attention to them? Yes it is, and yet as managers of the future we want to maintain a competitive edge and also to maximize the chances of making ourselves employable in the future. Analytical skills are key to knowledge management and provide us with a way to solve well-defined problems. We suggest that it is in the integration of analytical skills with the tacit skills we are exploring in this chapter that you will have that edge.

What is a skill of knowing?

To understand the notion of a skill of knowing, you may find the following example helpful. Imagine that you walk into a meeting without having prepared, a rare occurrence in the business world, we know! Your skills of knowing are about the know-how you bring to that meeting that allows you to quickly understand what is going on, to work out what your contribution might be and to adapt your behaviour in relation to what is happening in order to achieve your desired outcomes. In essence, it is your ability to decide what is relevant in this situation.

Let us explore another example that will be familiar to you. You need to prepare a presentation that addresses the issue of 'Why do we as an organization have such a high people turnover in our creative department?' You are making this presentation to the board in five days' time and have been with the company for two weeks. You want to make a good impression so you will present a possible solution to the problem. What do you do first? Who do you talk to? How do you find out the kind of knowledge that will help you achieve you objective? You need a solution to the high turnover and you need it quickly. It is your ability to determine relevance that will make or break you. In Chapters 3 and 4 we explored ways to gather data and create a framework. There is an old computing saying, 'garbage in, garbage out'. You will need to determine who is worth listening to, who has the kind of knowledge that you can trust and that you can use. Once you know that, you will need to decide what to highlight and what to leave behind. How do you do that? Do you have explicit tools available to help you maximize the potential for finding the solution that will get you the respect you want from the board?

Relevance is defined 'on-line' when choosing a particular path to pursue when gathering data for knowledge working, and also 'off-line' when reading written data and summarizing that which is important is some way. This is the skill that the knowledge manager brings to the knowledge management process. Morik (1991) argues for the distinction between knowledge and skill. Skill is unconscious, but can be made explicit enough to be learnt within a particular context. As you read written material for your presentation and as you decide that you will interview the head of your creative department, you are using the kind of skills that we are exploring in this chapter and the next.

Let us understand understanding

There is much theory that we could explore to inform us on how we make sense of all the events that go on in an average day at the office; you might like to reflect on what your particular 'average' day is like. We perform the incredible feats of cognition we mentioned earlier and that happens without involving other people. Now we want you to ask another question: How do you understand other people and how do others understand you?

5.2 What does it mean to understand?

Step 1   *Find someone else with whom to have a conversation.*

Step 2   *Think of a time when after struggling for to understand a particular idea or situation you suddenly understood exactly what that idea or situation was about.*

Step 3   *Describe that experience to your partner, concentrating on what the differences in your perception are in moving from confusion to understanding.*

Step 4   *Your partner will listen and take notes, asking any questions he or she thinks can help expand the detail of your experience.*

Step 5   *Your partner will then describe your experience back to you using YOUR words. He or she will stop when you let him or her know that the description is not accurate and suggest what to say instead. He or she will then continue the description incorporating your suggestions until you stop them again with more suggestions.*

Step 6   *Continue this process for five minutes and then swap roles.*

You may have found yourself having to stop your partner several times. This activity gives you permission to do in an explicit way something that our conversational norms rarely allow: interrupt and ask for accuracy. This process of understanding is key in any conversation and is crucial to successful knowledge acquisition. If I want to create an accurate model of a particular area of knowledge, I must be able to talk with people in such a way that, were they given the option, they would not interrupt me when I describe my understanding of their experience.

Understanding emerges in the following way: The nature of our bodies and our physical and cultural environment imposes a structure on our experience, in terms of natural dimensions. Recurrent experience leads to the formation of categories, which are experiential gestalts with those natural dimensions. We understand experience metaphorically when we use a gestalt from one domain of experience to structure experience in another domain.'
(Lakoff and Johnson, 1980a)

In exploring how we understand a key concept, we must consider is metaphor. What has metaphor got to do with understanding? Understanding one area of experience in terms of another, defines a metaphor and defines a key skill of knowing. Metaphorical understanding gives us a very practical skill to develop, which can allow us to acquire knowledge effectively. Try the activities below for a clear demonstration of this.

5.3 Metaphor primer

Think of one of the most complex areas of personal expertise you have. Imagine describing it to someone with no knowledge of the area at all. How would you do it? As soon as you spot yourself saying 'it's a bit like . . .' or something similar, you are engaging a metaphor. Try two or three different metaphors for aspects of your specialist knowledge. Try not to use a well-known existing metaphor – for example, in physics it has been common for many years to describe an atom as being a bit like a solar system with the nucleus as the sun and the electrons as planets. Do not use such a well-known metaphor.

5.4 Understanding others by discovering their knowledge metaphors

In order to take aspects of other people's knowledge on board, you must learn to uncover their hidden metaphors.

Step 1   *Find an opportunity to chat with someone at the coffee machine and ask them to choose a topic to talk about which they consider abstract in some way (e.g. the importance of learning to succeed in a job, what is important in a relationship, the essence of good government, planning). Ask them to talk about it. Assume everything they say is true.*

Step 2   *Make a mental note of the characteristics of the topic which seem to define it. For example, talking about learning, the person talking might say words like 'clarity', 'an end point', 'obstacles', 'stop along the way to reflect', 'when overloaded I can't learn'. As you hear details, think 'if this is true, what else has to be true about it?'*

Step 3   *Ask yourself, 'what have I come across in the physical world that has these characteristics and could be used to structure the topic?' This generates the metaphor:* Learning is (like) a journey. *A journey is an example of the source-path-goal schema (see 'Embodied image schemata' above).*

Step 4   *To check that you have an appropriate link, select a characteristic of your metaphor that you think might apply to the original topic and ask a question about it. For example:* Are there specific steps in reaching the end point of learning a particular subject?

Step 5   *When you have produced at least two structuring metaphors, take the opportunity to explain your new tool to your conversational partner. He or she might just be very grateful for the tip!*

The skill consists of the ability to bend your world view and adjust the way you categorize your experience. (Lakoff and Johnson, 1980a)

In doing Activity 5.4 you will have found out many interesting aspects of conversation and of the kind of know-how that is involved in understanding the way people structure what they know 'inside their heads'. For example, the effect of assuming that what was being said was true stopped you from making a judgement about what you heard. As you asked yourself 'what else has to be true?', you will have come up with images and possibilities to help you make sense of what you were listening to. The characteristics you were attending to will have formed themselves into the structure 'A is B': learning is a journey, or time is money, or words are containers. You will have defined the words you heard in terms of a more general structure which, in turn allows you to make predictions about what is not being said. Here are some examples of dialogues from our knowledge acquisition interviews in two different areas.

A cancer expert (E) and a knowledge engineer (KE) working with knowledge about what defines a 'good chemotherapy protocol':

KE: So your definition of a good protocol is those three things: less hospitalization, minimal constraints, minimum side effects?

E: Do you know the consumer association? When you buy something you need to know both the quality and the price. Quality equals efficiency, and price is side effects – the cost to the patient. The more desirable protocol is the protocol with the higher ratio of efficiency to price. It is very easy to ensure quality but the price is higher.

Next the interviewer follows the comparison made by the expert, and uses her language to gather the information which was not apparent in the first response:

KE: Included in the price are things like, length of time in hospital?

E: The price . . . mainly two different things. Price for society and price of the pain of the patient. The price of pain is the most important evaluation of the price and it is very difficult to evaluate. For example for breast cancer, hair loss for a woman is a high price, but for me not at all. There is a price for everything and it is very difficult to evaluate it.

Through the use of the expert's metaphor it is possible to gather more data about the topic of interest. Not all metaphors are so explicit and so easy to follow. It is important to notice that the experienced knowledge engineer will listen and explore the expert's language in this way, and that this is not normally done with awareness of the process. This is what we address in detail in the next chapter, providing a description of this process which will allow you to improve knowledge exploration skills even further.

Compare the previous example with the example below, a dialogue where the knowledge engineer was consciously using the skills of knowing we are looking at. The expert in this example is the deputy head of a school in England exploring the knowledge involved in planning his curriculum:

KE: So is the whole process like a path where you're seeing different walls as they succeed?

E: I think yes, but . . . I mean . . . I use the wall metaphor, because I see it as something that is being put down unnecessarily. I think that you can talk about limitations and boundaries. There is a boundary they will naturally reach even if you maximize their potential. There will be a limit at any particular moment in time as to where *they can get to*.

KE: Get to? Is it a journey?

E: Yes. very much so.

KE: So is it a journey? And the *it* here is learning? A journey where what you are doing is breaking down different walls that you come across?

E: It is almost as if you are on this journey, and it is almost as if you are carrying with you this wall that is around you, so although you may be going along on this journey, the wall will appear in front of you at some point, and it has been put there for various reasons: either by the child himself or by circumstance or by perceptions they've picked up from other people and that will unnaturally limit them. And it is actually breaking down that built up barrier so that they can actually carry on their journey to something that is more like what they can do.

KE: Who defines the journey?

E: If you want to think of the journey in terms of days, on any particular day. The journey itself will be defined not just by the barriers of the child but also in terms of their own stamina: given no barriers, how far can they actually travel on that day. And that depends on all sorts of things: how well they have been fed beforehand, whether or not they are fit and healthy. And if they are not then they are not going to progress very far along the way, because they haven't the mental capacity to do that. You can also look at it in terms of the physical, if the child is not feeling very well then they are going to want to have a rest along the way. And although they may be capable on an ideal day of travelling much further, you have to recognize that they've done what they can do under the circumstances.

KE: Where do you get to when you get to the end of this journey?

E: It is one those journeys that never ends. If you want to look at it in terms of purely schooling, you could say that the end of the journey is when they finish their exams. But I take a much broader view of education and that is that if you are lucky and you approach your life in the right way your journey never ends – you continually learn.

KE: So, when you talk about this journey, what can you see?

E: I can almost see it as someone from the Wild West, if you like. And they are setting off from the east and you've got this enormous continent in front of you. And it may take a lifetime to get across it and even when you get across it and you suddenly reach the ocean, there is still more of this journey to do and you just keep on going, there is no limit. It is very much an individual journey and you can experience parts with people, parts on your own, experience part of it in a huge crowd of people; you may come down for a while in a particular place and then get restless again and want to go on. You may start off in a particular direction and you may decide that you want to go on and explore in another. Head off south or something.

KE: What is your role as a teacher in this journey that your children make?

E: It is very simple. It is to enable them to want to travel; no one is going to get very far if they don't want to. They've got to want to travel in this journey of learning and they also have to have with them the things that will enable them to travel independently. They are never going to get very far if they are dependent on someone driving the car for them! Yeah? So it's giving them what they need to do their journey, and you can look at that in terms of skills mostly, on the journey they will acquire knowledge, but the knowledge is not vital for doing the journey, it's the skills that are vital for doing the journey.

Notice that we started with a statement where the metaphors were not explicit and that it is only after the questions were asked which directed the expert's attention to the knowledge structure that it could be jointly explored in an explicit way. See Appendix 1 for the complete annotated interview.

His comments after the interview might motivate you even more to learn what we are offering in this book. The expert identified a number of uses for the metaphors which he discovered. He stated that it would provide a tool for explaining to new teachers the strategies he uses in planning tasks for his children. They would have 'a sense of the kinds of questions they need to ask, the ordering of questions they need to ask when planning a lesson'. He specifically said that had he been asked for a procedure he would not have been able to give one. He concluded:

E: It is incredibly powerful. If I was to sit down and talk to you about what I do, or the processes that go through my mind when I'm planning something. Partly now because I am so used to doing it that I don't consciously think of how I do it. They are done unconsciously, done without thinking about them. It would have been impossible for me to explain to you in such a vivid way what I do, it would have been very vague. And I was aware that when we started to acquire a metaphor to use as a framework, that then made everything very clearly outlined. I was able then to see how it all fitted together. And also having had a picture, you can see where the gaps were in my explanation of what I was doing. And you were also able to seize on parts of my metaphor, parts of my picture, and say I can understand the principle of what happens there, but what happens to this particular bit, how do you remove this particular brick. So it gave us both a framework which we could use to bridge that enormous gap between what I do and your understanding of it. I felt it was a very powerful way in which to crystallize in my own mind what I do, or making me conscious of what I do. Whereas had I sat down and tried to make myself conscious, it would have taken a long time.

MORE INFO . . .

Metaphor

The fundamental nature of metaphor 'is understanding and experiencing one kind of thing in terms of another'. The way we talk about things presupposes metaphors we do not *consciously* perceive. We act on the basis of these; *they are not just a matter of language*, and are not fully definable independently of the context in which they occur. Through metaphor we understand what is relevant in a communication. This understanding is dependent on context and is unconscious.

SKILLS OF KNOWING

How do you conceive of a brilliant idea?

Here is another way for you to explore understanding and to begin to work at a different level of language than the obvious content of a message. Take the statement 'to conceive a brilliant idea'.

Part of the statement implies that *there is an idea* – the existence of the idea is the content of the statement, what is being talked about. The statement also makes it sound like *an idea is an organism that can be conceived*. This is the process in the statement, how the idea is being talked about. Understanding in each of these ways will lead you as a knowledge manager to pursue different aspects of the knowledge. If both *conceive* and *idea* are targeted in what you hear, you will start a process where a number of things can be noticed:

- There is a conflict between the conventional meanings of 'conceive' and 'idea'.
- The expression could have no meaning, though we assume it does. Sperber and Wilson (1986) have found that this is a fundamental law of conversation.
- If it has a meaning, what could it be?

There are a number of choices to resolve this conflict. Define the context, make sense of the expression by deciding that if an *idea is an organism* then it can be *conceived* and if *it is an organism*, a number of hypotheses are generated which you may choose to explore.

Some questions which present themselves are: Can it die? What kind of an organism is it? How is it born? What can it do? The answers would tell us about the structure of the content, how the content is understood.

We can use this process of developing metaphor explicitly to structure an area of knowledge and to anticipate missing properties. Awareness of this linguistic process has to be taught because, as was said previously, we do not process these metaphors consciously and an explicit method for what to target in language can be useful for acquiring high-quality knowledge. We explore this technique in more depth in Chapter 6. Its significance to you as a manager is clear: it allows you to know how to ask pertinent questions and that means high-quality knowledge. You may want to revisit Chapter 3 once you have grasped this chapter and the next.

Uncovering metaphors

A method to identify underlying metaphors is necessary because the structure and instances used can be very specific to each individual. You need to be able to generate a system of metaphors that are unique to each area of knowledge you explore, and this can then be used to determine what is relevant to your intended purpose.

What all this means to you in your daily working life is simple. To be able to create, acquire, store and use knowledge that can allow you to do your job more effectively, you need to be aware of the many ways in which you make sense of the world around you. This goes beyond the realm of psychologists being interested in the mind and how it works. We know that you may well not have time to be interested in that. This is significant to you because it will allow you to be more effective at the one thing that is at the core of any knowledge management activity: communication. As we demonstrated when we discussed the different approaches to knowledge that managers of today may have (Chapter 1), knowledge is characterized by a high degree of diversity. Honed skills of knowing will start you on the journey to genuinely work with diversity. It will help you learn that effective performance comes from your ability to develop different perspectives, understand them and let go of your need to change them. Chapter 6 will provide a step-by-step guide to different knowing skills. Enjoy it by all means, and remember that there is a very tough business reason for enjoying the next chapter: knowledge is the currency of the next millennium.

Wisdom develops when people can talk about their differences without the need to change the other person.
(Gregory Bateson, 1972)

Summary

We must bother with honing our skills of knowing if we want to become expert knowledge managers because these are a fundamental building block to support and enhance our analytical skills. Effective knowledge management requires that we think in a variety of different ways to fit the increasing complexity of our working lives. A practical understanding of how you create meaning in your experience, how you understand, is key to your ability to create knowledge. In this chapter we have explored how metaphor can provide an account of how we understand the world. The body is a metaphor for the mind and we can determine what is relevant in a knowledge area in relation to the functioning of our body in the world. So our abstract thoughts are metaphorically structured in terms of concrete experience. In exploring new topics, a knowledge manager has to find meaning in a subject he or she does not yet know. We have provided an explicit description of this process which is often not unpacked beyond telling the novice manager to 'decide which are the important concepts' in a given area and acquire the relevant knowledge to achieve agreed objectives.

Learning review

Some questions to help you review your learning from this chapter might be:

1 If you had to write an executive summary of this chapter, what would you write?
2 What might be a headline for your favourite newspaper to describe this chapter?
3 What has changed in your knowledge map as a result of this chapter?
4 What is the relevance of metaphor?
5 How is a skill of knowing the same or different from know-how?
6 What is one question you can formulate for yourself, which you now want answered having finished this chapter?

6 Your skills of knowing toolbag

Our objectives

- To give you a set of practical tools to hone your tacit skills in knowledge management.
- To help you expand you notion of literacy.
- To help you learn how to learn, thus improving your ability to create knowledge.
- To provide a 'workout' for honing our skills of knowing.

As we look ahead to longer and increasingly discontinuous lives, through which we can expect to move from place to place and from task to task, it is clear that the congruence of different tasks, the recognition that a particular skill can be applied in the new context, is what make the transfer of learning possible. (Bateson, 1994)

In this chapter we practise and define key skills of knowing, your 'know-how bag'. There are different types of literacy we need to develop and which put together will give us honed knowing skills. Successful knowledge management initiatives carry explicit statements about the processes which the organization puts in place for these initiatives to succeed. A subtext, often hidden under the heading 'creating a knowledge sharing culture', is that individuals need to be at a stage in their own development where they are willing and able to put their knowledge behind the initiative. Our toolbag will help you contribute to your organization's initiatives in a way that supports a knowledge sharing culture.

An overarching goal of the skills of knowing toolbag is to help you be conscious of what you are doing when you acquire knowledge. This will mean holding beliefs which are supportive of your efforts and which will allow you, for example, to let go of the need for clear objectives when the kind of knowledge you are acquiring or using demands that you do so. In short, what follows is a course on thinking in ways you may not have called thinking in the past.

MORE INFO . . .

A model of best practice from management development

Roffey Park Management Institute is researching the cognitive abilities of management development professionals and we have presented our initial findings at the Research Conference of the Association For Management, Education and Development (1997). The content of this chapter is partly grounded on this research.

As you read this, are you talking to yourself to help you understand? Experiencing certain images and sounds from your past? Or trying to predict what will come next? At another level, are you moving towards clarity or away from confusion? Are you making decisions about how these ideas are similar or different from your own?

Your answers to these questions reflect the way you think. This is what we are currently researching. Thinking is a very rich subject, (e.g. Bandler and Grinder, 1975, 1979; Bretto, 1990; Dilts et al., 1980; Laborde, 1988), so we have focused on a specific form of thinking, knowledge transfer skills or bridging.

There is something you know. It has no obvious connection to the field of management. Yet, you are able to bring it in to your professional practice and create the necessary connections. It is *that* skill that we refer to as bridging. We have started our research with an exploration of the ways that management development professionals use what they know. How do they make decisions about what is relevant and what is not relevant when they are working with people? Some developers excel at this. By appropriate interpretation, initially irrelevant experiences become appropriate for use within the context of work. For example, the use of coaching in sports to illuminate management skills. It is our intention to create a model of how people use life experiences to illuminate and enrich their professional practice. The data we have elicited to date has generated a richness well beyond any expectations. (Funes, 1998).

Managing knowledge as a management skill requires that you understand how to acquire, generate, access, integrate and, a favourite word of knowledge management gurus, leverage it. Underlying this kind of language is the assumption that knowledge is an object that can be acquired, manipulated in some way and that we can finally find a one-to-one correspondence between its function and our business needs. Much in the same way as we might understand that the function of our personal organizer is to organize and that when we need to be effective organizers, a high leverage point is to access our personal organizer and integrate it into our professional practice.

It is dangerous to think of this shortcut of language as the reality of knowledge management. In our rapidly changing world we run a serious risk of accumulating a great deal of knowledge, in the same way that we accumulate objects in our homes. We may forget to ask a fundamental question about the knowledge we have accumulated: Is it still relevant knowledge? It could be argued that a core meta-skill, the skill behind all knowledge skills, is our willingness to know that knowledge is ephemeral, like The Little Prince's rose, and that the metaphor of knowledge as object is more a reflection of our need for stability than of reality. Einstein would not have been able to stand on the shoulders of giants and move the domain of physics forward if he had thought of knowledge as a solid object. It is in the nature of what we know that we change our mind about what we know. In sum, the metaskill is 'our willingness to accumulate the experience of having been wrong so many times that we are still open to learning' as Mary Catherine Bateson put it at a recent conference on intuition. So, the point of leverage for you as the manager of the future is not in acquiring knowledge. It is in having the skills to keep acquiring relevant knowledge and letting go of irrelevant knowledge.

This is not to say that *all* your knowledge has to be continually changing. Much of our existing knowledge can be utilized and recombined to give us a new ways of knowing. But there is a stage of not knowing how to put it all together that comes before a new reconfiguration of our knowledge. Being comfortable with both having knowledge and not having a clue is key to effective knowledge management.

Perceptual literacy

You are the quality of your perception. (Claxton, 1996)

What is perception? And why is it important to become literate in it? We use our senses every minute of our lives to take in the world around us, and we are designed to do this without conscious attention. There are times, however, when we have it brought home in a painfully clear way just how much data our senses take in. You may remember thinking when you learnt to drive: 'I will never be able to take in all that this instructor is asking me to notice!' The road and its signs were like a foreign language, the car felt like you had just been transported to the USS Enterprise control room, and this constant voice next to you giving you directions. If you add to all of that your thoughts and feelings which you will have attained to some degree, you start to get a sense of why, if we may momentarily be allowed to treat perception as a homunculus inside our head. Perception is selective and judgemental. It jumps to conclusions before it has complete information and ignores data which may be counter to the conclusion.

Framed in this way, it can be very obvious that a great deal of our organizational problems can be put down to problems of perception. Nowhere is this more evident than in knowledge management. We operate from our own perceptual filters (some of which were explored in Chapter 1) as we continually interact with people in a great variety of situations. How we act in the meeting with the expert accountant, for example, is determined to a large extent by our perception of that accountant and that situation. Perception is all about interpreting sensory information.

An appreciation of this process is a key skill of knowing because in managing knowledge your perception, and particularly your perceptual biases, will determine your choice of relevant knowledge to acquire or to utilize in a given situation. It follows that to learn to enhance your perceptual literacy will lead to sharpening up your attention and seeing beyond snap judgements. This will buy accuracy and a closer match of knowledge items to the needs of a given situation.

MORE INFO . . .

The hare and the tortoise

Guy Claxton (1997) uses this metaphor to distinguish two distinct ways of being. In hare-mode we rush to rationally solve problems and think analytically, and in tortoise-mode we allow ill-defined problems to be held in our mind while our unconscious works on them. Claxton reviews the latest research in cognitive science that suggests that intelligence can increase when we think less (in the rational mode). He argues for the need to develop a mode of thinking that appreciates and welcomes ambiguity, paradox and 'the tinkering towards the truth that characterizes a child's mind'. We can have rigour and certainty when we address particular kinds of problems and issues. Other problems require that we are comfortable 'hanging out in the fog' of not knowing. He encourages us to perceive beyond what we expect to see, to take time to see beyond the obvious, if we want to learn new ways of knowing to help us manage the complex demands of our working lives.

We experience the world through our senses. Such input is called sensory data. Sensory data is transmitted to our brain, which in turn makes guesses about the meaning of this data. So perception cannot be separated from thought. The judgement of whether something is good, bad or indifferent has already been made before we consciously consider it. We see things as we are, not as they are, as some important person once said.

6.1 Perception is organized and meaningful

Write five short statements about your perception of these four boxes:

Your statements will tell you about your perceptual filters. Perceptually you will have discovered something of how you make decisions. Check what you have written against the decision factors filter we explored in Chapter 1. Are these boxes the same? Two pairs of different boxes? What did you consider the the relationship between these boxes to be?

Perception is selective

You will probably not have noticed that the final sentence in the previous activity had the word 'the' repeated. Our expectations delete sensory data that does not seem immediately relevant to our hypotheses of what is there. Time is particularly good at reducing the selectivity and penetration of our perception. We have to allow ourselves extra time to work round the quick judgements of our perception. It is designed to be selective, but for effective knowledge acquisition and use we have to learn to go beyond the obvious.

6.2 Perception is context-dependent

Step 1   *Find someone to have a conversation about something that happened at the office last year.*

Step 2   *Now pretend your are Murphy, from Murphy's law. If anything can go wrong it will. In your mind's eye filter your conversation through the following two statements:*

○ *Life is a struggle.*
○ *Change is painful.*

Step 3   *Have a conversation while holding these statements in mind. Do this for five minutes at the most.*

Step 4   *Now it is your turn to be Pollyanna:*

○   *Life is a journey.*
○   *An opportunity to learn.*
○   *Change is a natural process.*

Step 5   *Talk about the same event while holding these statements in mind. Do this for as long as you want for it will be much more enjoyable than being Murphy!*

You will have discovered some key differences between the two. What we ask you to notice is that the event remained the same. The context for the conversation changed and the Murphy context directed your attention to one particular set of data and the Pollyanna context directed your attention to something else that was also present in the same event.

Perception

We cannot overstress the importance of these activities to your understanding of perception. The implications are many but the 'what' we want to highlight here is that human beings are always attending to something and can choose where they direct their attention. An analogy for this process is our perception of those visual illusions so widely used by psychologists, where a single picture can seem to be two totally different images. We can choose which one to see once we have seen both. In exploring in Chapter 5 how we understand, we looked at the evidence that abstract reasoning uses metaphors of the physical world (see also Funes, 1995).

What this means to your practical day-to-day knowledge management is that you can develop your perceptual ability to distinguish between an objective and accurate description of your experience, and your attempts to interpret it with your perceptual filters. It is your ability to do this which will ultimately allow you gain new knowledge and utilize your existing knowledge effectively.

6.3 Paying attention

Step 1 *Find a place to sit where you can be undisturbed for fifteen minutes. This may seem a long time to spend on an activity, like this, but trust us – it will be worth it.*

Step 2 *Sit with your back straight but not rigid (see physical literacy below) and close your eyes.*

Step 3 *Breathing naturally, notice the point of contact between the air, as it comes in, and your body. Your attention is directed to the air as it enters your nostrils.*

Step 4 *Bring your awareness to the sense of touch of the air as it passes through your body. In and out.*

Step 5 *Park your attention like a cat watching birds flying, it does not fly with them, it just watches them fly by. It just stays alert watching.*

Step 6 *Keep your attention at one precise point (the nostrils, or your stomach as the breath goes in and out) and notice the sensation of the breath as it flows in and out of your body.*

Step 7 *If your attention strays bring it back, noting to yourself: 'breathing in and breathing out'.*

Step 8 *This is your task for the next fifteen minutes. You will notice thoughts arising, feelings arising, sensation arising. You will note these and come back to your point of attention for your breath.*

Step 9 *After a while you will notice sounds outside that had gone unnoticed, patterns of images in your mind, you will watch them fly by and come back to your point of attention. Noticing the richness of sensations of your breath as it goes in and out. Nothing to do, just being aware of what is moment to moment.*

Step 10   *You may choose to set an alarm to mark your time doing this exercise. As the alarm rings it will give you information about how well you are attending to your task. If you jump up, your attention was not on your breathing it had gone flying with one of those thoughts. And that is okay. It is all information, no judgements, no right or wrongs.*

Doing this activity regularly will help you develop your perceptual literacy. Those of you familiar with the martial arts will know about the origins of this approach. In some circles it is called mindfulness training. We use it here to help us develop our ability to perceive what we know, to become more aware of what we might need to know in a given context and to increase our ability to notice the difference between sensory data and our judgements about that data.

 And yet the central survival skill is surely to pay attention and respond to changing circumstances, to learn and adapt, to fit into new environments beyond the safety of the temple precincts. (Bateson, 1994)

Conversational literacy

Conversational literacy is our ability to explore the world beyond the words we hear. In a sense, the distinctions we are making in this chapter about different types of literacy are quite artificial. They are necessary to help us highlight particular aspects of skills of knowing, but are categories with a high degree of overlap. We need our perceptual literacy to notice what goes on beyond the words we hear in a conversation. That said, we will assume for the purpose of illustration, that we can develop our conversational literacy independently.

Conversational literacy is about learning a set of patterns that provide pragmatic information about how a speaker's model of the world is structured and which go beyond just being aware of what the speaker is talking about. We refer to the former as the structure of language and the latter as the content. So we now move on to study grammar with a difference – the grammar of knowledge transfer.

MORE INFO . . .

What is neuro-linguistics?

Neuro-linguistics, originally known as neuro-linguistic programming (NLP) (Bandler and Grinder, 1975, 1979; Bretto, 1990; Dilts et al., 1980) is a technique for describing subjective experience. Though not without controversy (Graunke and Roberts, 1985; Gumm et al., 1982; Salas et al., 1989; Yeager, 1985) it provides explicit methods for understanding thinking patterns. According to NLP, human beings construct models of reality based on data collected through the use of their perceptual systems. Neuro-linguistic programming then assumes that different people pay more attention to different types of perceptual information when they come to interpret their experience.

A basic presupposition of the approach is that 'As modellers, we are not interested in whether what we offer you is true or not. It doesn't have to an actual representation of the world, we are only interested in what works.' (Bandler and Grinder, 1979). That is, as the ideas are applied, effectiveness is measured by how closely the results obtained match the desired outcomes. The approach is being used with some success in business, therapy and sports. It tries to describe the subjective experience of individuals who excel at a particular behaviour or skill in a way that is easily learnable by others, and so has been called a way of modelling excellence. The patterns that we explore in this section have their origin in this approach.

Sense language

We take information from the external world through the five senses: sight, hearing, touch, taste and smell (referred to in academic circles as modalities). If we assume that the senses are used internally to process and store information, we have a clear and practical way to make guesses about what is going on inside someone else's head. Let us look at some examples of what to attend to in conversation to become literate beyond words and to be able to acquire high-quality knowledge from those around you.

Sight

Picture, clear, focus, perspective, see, flash, bright, outlook, spectacle, glimpse, preview, short-sighted, distinguish, illustrate, delineate, paint, cloud, clarify, graphic, show, reveal, expose, screen.

Hearing

Tune, note, accent, ring, shout, growl, tone, sound, hear, say, ask, harmonize, key, muffle, rattle.

Touch and motion

Touch, handle, throw, shock, impact, sharpen, impress, strike, grapple with, getting a handle on, tangible, forward, backward, behind.

It is useful to target these sense-based terms in your expert's speech and writing, feeding them back to the expert to ensure understanding. You can then point out the term explicitly to the expert to access the metaphors being used.

For example, in the statement 'what I see is that this task is complex' we target the term [see] and you can then ask 'how do you see that?' This helps the expert focus on how he or she is representing the complex task.

6.4 Spotting the sense language

Take a newspaper and look at one of the longer features. Ignore the subject, just look for the way that sense-based words are used throughout the article. Does the writer have a bias towards one of the senses? Would it make any difference to the feeling of the article if there were a different bias?

Sense properties

Each sense deals with certain properties of the object under study (called submodalities in the jargon (Bandler and Macdonald, 1988)). As I form a mental picture of something, it has certain characteristics that are independent of the picture's content. Imagine a real picture hanging on a wall. It may be an image of a skiing scene – this is the content. It has, however, certain characteristics: the colours that have been used to paint it, the frame it has around it, the clarity of the image, the location of the picture on the wall, etc. – its properties. Sense properties provide directions to be investigated when exploring an expert's knowledge. The lists below show some examples.

Sight

Colour/black and white, brightness, contrast, focus, texture, detail, size, distance, shape, border, location, movement, orientation, singular image, associated/dissociated, proportion, dimension.

Hearing

Location, pitch, tonality, melody, inflection, volume, tempo, rhythm, duration, mono/stereo.

Touch and motion

Quality, intensity, location, movement, direction, speed, duration.

There are a set of questions that can help us get to these properties, which we list below (adapted from Bandler and MacDonald, 1988).

Sight

- Is the image you see in colour, in black and white, or a mixture of both?
- Are the colours vivid or washed out?
- Is the image you can see brighter or duller than normal?
- What is the contrast like? High or low?
- Is the image sharp in focus, is it fuzzy or blurry?
- Is the image smooth or roughly textured?
- Are there background and foreground details?
- Do you see the details as part of the whole or do you have to shift perspective to see them?
- How big is the picture?
- How far is the image?
- What shape is the picture?
- Is there a border or do edges fade out? What is the border like?
- Where is the image located in space? Show me with both hands where you see the image.

- Is it a movie? Is it still?
- How rapid is the movement? Faster or slower than normal?
- Is the image stable?
- What direction does it move in?
- Do you see yourself? Or is it as if you were there?
- Is there one image or more than one?
- Do you see the images sequentially or simultaneously?

Hearing

- Do you hear the voice as if coming from inside or outside?
- Where does the sound originate?
- Is it high pitched or low pitched?
- Is the pitch higher or lower than normal?
- What is the tonality: nasal, full and rich, thin, grating?
- Is it monotone or melodic?
- Which parts are stressed?
- How loud is it?
- Is it fast or slow?
- Does it have a beat or cadence?
- Is it continuous or intermittent?
- Do you hear the sound in one side, both sides, or is it all around you?

Touch and motion

- How would you describe the feeling in your body: tingling, warm, cold, relaxed, tense?
- How strong is the sensation?
- Where is the feeling in your body?
- Is there movement in the sensation?
- How long does the sensation last?
- What is the texture?

Sense- and property-based language allows us to explore the way knowledge is based on experience. It gives an insight into the way experts structure what they know in terms of particular experiences. It helps us understand the internal images they have constructed to organize what they know.

Having established an initial picture, it is useful to explore these properties to get more detail and start constructing the higher-level structures that may be present in the knowledge area. Clarifying which sense properties apply helps the expert clarify how they are representing knowledge internally, so the metaphors being used can emerge.

The key to working at this level is in paying close attention to the actual words used rather than the meaning they have in the context they are being used. The aim is to listen for the patterns. Once these are identified, it is possible to use the sense properties to explore further.

For example, if someone says 'I have to build up this theory', 'build up' is targeted as an example of a feeling term. It is possible to then ask, 'Which direction are you building up in?' or 'What is the speed you are building the theory at?', thus starting to explore other properties of this particular sense-based term to get more detail about how the person talking thinks of their theory.

Probing the model

The expert will not always find it easy to come out with a clear picture of what he or she wants to get across. In interviewing techniques, the model is often explored by asking for a specific situation or example of a given concept being discussed. An indirect way of accessing examples and thus sense-based language is to ask questions that probe the nature of the expert's model.

Useful cues are:

- use of spatial/directional terms (e.g. 'the meaning is right there *in* the words')
- referring to an action or process as if it were an object or thing (e.g. inflation is crippling me)
- detail of action or relationship isn't defined (e.g. 'as I *think about* making a diagnosis')
- noun or object isn't specified (e.g. 'you just do *that* and then you have your solution')
- two different things are made equivalent (e.g. 'the test results mean failure')
- assumptions made in part of the sentence (e.g. 'the solution is built up a bit at a time' assumes that the solution is being built/there is a solution)
- statements identifying rules or limits (e.g. 'you *can't* diagnose the fault without the test')
- broad generalizations (e.g. 'it is always the result').

You can then ask questions probing these usages. For example:

- How, what, where, when specifically?
- How do you know that x means y?
- What else could it mean?
- What would happen if you did/didn't?
- Are there any exceptions?
- What stops you?
- How is x significant?
- What does x accomplish for you?

These questions are equally effective when exploring the knowledge of an expert and as guides to analysis of written data. They provide stimulation for sense-based language and can be freely used in conversation. This line of questioning explores perceived links in the speaker's model of the world. If the speaker can then access the sense-based language which generated the links it is possible to get through to the underlying picture that the expert has in mind. This in turn can generate the structure used in the more abstract levels of knowledge, that of real world and body metaphor as explored in Chapter 5.

If we can understand others in the way we have presented here, the knowledge we acquire will be high quality and the model we develop of that knowledge will reflect the structure given to it by those who have the expertise. Also, given that a lot of the knowledge that we have about our management practice is tacit knowledge or know-how, it is essential to have smart ways to acquire it to help us bring into the open.

6.5 Getting further into the model

Step 1   *Imagine you are talking to some colleagues about a current business issue.*

Step 2   *Your task is to talk about your subject stressing one of the following categories:*

- ○ *Universals: all, every, each, always, forever.*
- ○ *Imperatives: must, have to, should.*
- ○ *Nouns: they, managers, it, company policy, that.*
- ○ *Verbs: processing, enjoying, hating, thinking.*
- ○ *Limitations: can't, mustn't, shouldn't.*
- ○ *Comparisons: better, worse, more, less.*

Step 3   *Spend one minute on each category. Jot down what you said to the others. Make it like dialogue in a novel, not a report. Stop and check how you feel before moving on to the next. What was the feeling generated by each? (excitement, carelessness, aggression . . .) Write it down before moving on to the next question.*

Step 4   *What was the effect of using each approach? How easy was it to do?*

This activity will give you an indication of the language patterns you prefer to use to structure what you know. In order to have a body of knowledge about anything we need to generalize, distort and delete sensory data to create a consistent model. We simplify when we apply structure and we have personal preferences as to the language patterns we use to for this process. This activity will have told you about the patterns you regularly use, those that you felt comfortable with, and those that aren't yet part of your armoury, those you found tough to use.

The expert knowledge manager must be competent at the detection and use of sense-based language and sense properties, and at probing links in the expert's model, because this will allow the collection of high-quality knowledge, grounded in the expert's everyday experience. You will also be able to structure your own subjective experience with greater awareness, thus enabling you to access what you know more effectively as circumstances require it.

There is a lot more that could be covered about the structure of language beyond the immediate content of the words used. The level of conversational literacy you will achieve by practising the activities in this section will be more than sufficient for honing your knowledge skills. If you are interested in this area in more depth, explore the 'more info' boxes in this chapter and the previous one, and follow up the references for more in-depth study.

Acquiring planning knowledge in teaching

An extended example in Appendix 1 demonstrates how this approach can be used in a real conversation to acquire knowledge from an expert. Conversational literacy in action!

Mental literacy

Mental literacy is about how effective we are at managing our mind to help us achieve the results we want to achieve in our knowledge management activities. In this section we explore two strategies for managing the mind. Bracketing and bridging are metaphors for mind-managing. The ability to act as if something was happening in our internal world allows us greater flexibility in gathering data and creating knowledge about our environment. Mental literacy helps us to increase mind associations and generate more comprehensive knowledge maps.

A bridging strategy

This strategy gives you a way to practise understanding connections between different areas of knowledge:

1 Have an experience, selected on the basis of strong personal interest
2 Think back to that experience as if you were watching a film in your mind's eye.
3 Ask yourself:
   - 'what is the essence of this experience?' or/and
   - 'how can I make sense of this?' or/and
   - 'what labels can I put on this?'

4 Place this experience somewhere in your mind, along with the meaning and connections you have made.

Now you have gathered the data, you can allow some time to go by before the next stages:

5 Imagine you are explaining a difficult concept from your area of expertise to your Chief Executive.
6 Decide on your goal for the conversation: Tell yourself 'what he needs now is . . .' Fill in the blank with a short sentence.
7 Retrieve the memory of your previous experience and the meanings and connections you made.
8 Ask yourself 'In what way is the point I am trying to get across the same as my relived experience?' 'How can it help me put the concept across to the boss?'
9 Note down three ways in which you could use it to help you achieve your conversational goal.

Our ability to combine what we know in new ways is fundamental to knowledge management. We create new knowledge that way. This bridging strategy will help you become more effective at connecting what you know in new ways.

A bracketing strategy

The philosopher Husserl conceived the notion of human beings 'bracketing off' the 'whatness' of data to allow ourselves to start looking at how data came into being in our consciousness. This is one of those techniques that is a lot easier to describe by example. So:

1 Become aware of your hypotheses about a given situation. For example, What are your generalizations about the accountant you may be meeting to acquire some knowledge from?
2 In your mind's eye put brackets around your hypotheses. This means be aware of them, but suspend them (in the sense of 'hang in front') for examination.
3 Choose an experience that will help you explore your hypotheses and consider only what is available in the experience. Apply your perceptual literacy learning to help you do this.
4 Unbracket the hypotheses and notice what is confirmed and what is not after having had the experience.

The skill is about holding in abeyance the classifications and constructs we impose on our perceiving. (Heron, 1996)

There is an assumption underlying this strategy that people can be aware of their hypotheses about a given area of knowledge and that they can choose to put brackets around these in their virtual world of mind. Applying bracketing to knowledge acquisition allows us to collect more accurate data and manage our internal preconceptions about what we perceive.

Let us revisit the thoughts of Purposeful Paula to see bracketing in action: As Paula would say: 'I am aware that I'm making certain assumptions about Mr Roberts and not all of them may be helpful. What are they? Let me write them down. That he will be a "typical" accountant; that he will talk in jargon and I won't understand him; that he will be arrogant; that it will take too long to get to the useful information I need. So, step one in bracketing is to become aware of my hypotheses. Consider it done. What next? Bracket them. I am now aware of what I am assuming and I can choose to put brackets around them, as if I was putting them in a box, the content of which I know well. Okay, done. What next? Go to that meeting and pay attention to what actually happens, keep my senses open and sharp and notice what happens rather than my interpretation of what happens. After I come out of the meeting I can take everything out of the box and compare my box contents with my notes of the meeting.'

The key to the technique is to allow ourselves to consciously hold hypotheses and beliefs about our experience (rather than keep them in the shadowlands of the mind), and suspend judgement for a bounded chunk of time so we can compare and contrast sensory data with our hypotheses about the world.

MORE INFO . . .

Being in flow

Psychologist Mihaly Csikszentmihalyi (1996) has dedicated his career to researching optimal experience. He asks the question: What are the qualities necessary to perform at our best? His works spans decades in which he has carried out in-depth research interviews with a huge variety of people. Optimal experience is found in a state he calls *flow*. His research has shown that 'The flow experience was described in almost identical terms regardless of the activity that produced it'. Flow has the following characteristics:

- clear goals
- immediate feedback
- balance between challenge and skill level
- action and awareness are one
- consciousness contain only what is relevant in the present moment
- a failure-free zone
- a self-consciousness free zone
- timeshifting
- activity is an end in itself.

A way of thinking about the skills of knowing presented in this chapter is that they may help us access this flow state. Flow as a state for managing knowledge implies that we would be in the optimum state for peak performance. Honed skills of knowing enhance the likelihood of being in flow and have our body-mind support our knowledge managing efforts. Look at Mihaly Csikszentmihalyi's latest book *Finding Flow: The Psychology of Engagement of Everyday Life* (1997) for a series of stimulating challenges to help people find flow in everyday life. You will have to bridge the book content to knowledge managment skills.

We end this section with two activities that will help you to use your mind, generating an internal state which is supportive of managing knowledge in your organization. Two activities that may help you find flow (see 'more info' above).

6.6 Use your mind for a change

Step 1   *Identify something you are physically good at, for example, dancing, juggling, swimming.*

Step 2   *In your mind's eye get into the physiology of that activity. Choose a time when you particularly enjoyed that activity. See, hear and feel what it is like. Be there.*

NEW SKILLS PORTFOLIO

Step 3 Now identify a 'bad state' (e.g. being driven, cannot stop) and get into the physiology of what that feels like. Select a time and rerun it in the same way as for 2 above.

Step 4 Get back into the positive activity and while you keep on re-experiencing what that is like, bring back that 'bad state'. Notice how it has changed.

6.7 Choosing a state of mind

Step 1 Select the state you want to have easily available (confidence, relaxation, fun).

Step 2 Identify a specific time when you had that state.

Step 3 In you imagination put yourself fully back into that experience. Where are you? What are you doing? What can you see around you? Any sounds? Where in your body are the feelings located? Allow yourself to relive that experience fully.

Step 4 When you know that you are fully there, choose a sound and image and the specific quality of a feeling which would without doubt get you back in this experience. Ask yourself: if there were one thing that would get me back here, what would that be? We call this a self-anchor for that experience.

Step 5 Test your self-anchor and notice how quickly you can get that state back.

A few words on physical literacy and emotional literacy

It is beyond the scope of this book to look in great detail at our emotions and our bodies. It is important, however, to mention that an increase in your physical and emotional literacy will improve your effectiveness in managing knowledge. Our body and emotions support us in our ability to work with knowledge. We must think of the whole body, not just the brain. If we learn to use our body effortlessly, energy will be freed up for thinking and structuring knowledge. The Alexander technique can teach you to free up this energy in a way that does not require you to take time out of your working day. (The Society of Teachers of the Alexander Technique in London will provide you with information.)

We also need to understand that knowledge does not exist independently of our emotions. The need to become more emotionally literate in our organizational life has been highlighted by Daniel Goleman (1995) in his book on emotional intelligence. Know that your emotions are part of you and that they need to develop as well as your intelligence to help you manage knowledge effectively and creatively. The role of laughter in this context cannot be overestimated (Funes, 1997). It is possible to laugh your way to insight and knowledge and there is a trend to bring humour and laughter in the workplace that indicates that organizations are beginning to realize the potential of emotional intelligence to improve performance. See Annette Goodheart's *Laughter Therapy* (1994) for an entertaining exposition of this.

Ha-ha can lead to ah-*ha*! (Arthur Koestler, 1964)

This toolbag is designed to teach you to think in new ways, to allow you to be more flexible and more able to handle the information superhighway as if it were a friendly country road. The activities are designed to allow your mind to enter a different time zone and bring all of you into your knowledge management activities. Rechtschaffen (1996) refers to this underlying skill of knowing as timeshifting. When we timeshift we can slow down and be comfortable with 'not having a clue'. A honed ability to timeshift (Rechtschaffen, 1996) may well be what saves the human race from final burnout from information overload. The extent to which we are comfortable with not knowing will determine the effectiveness of our skill of knowing toolbag. Paradoxically, our ability to know seems to be determined by our willingness to not know. We can never know it all; effective knowledge management is about knowing how to obtain and use the knowledge that is relevant in a given context. To that end we must always be willing to let go of the old and trust our ability to acquire the new.

Summary

We have explored three types of literacy: perceptual, conversational and mental. We have offered you a series of activities that will allow you to develop you skills of knowing, the tacit knowledge that is needed in order to acquire knowledge through learning. Your skills of knowing toolbag will support your application of the analytical skills of the previous chapters and allow you to become an expert knowledge manager. We have mentioned that the three ways of knowing we have explored are only the tip of the iceberg. Emotional and physical literacy must also be developed to allow us acquire knowledge in an integrated and congruent way. The more of us that is involved in the process the more likely it is that the knowledge we manage will be complete and, therefore, more reliable in its use for a given purpose.

Learning review

Some questions to help you review your learning from this chapter might be:

1 If you were to tell a colleague about this chapter what would you say?
2 What is the one nugget that you may find yourself quoting over coffee?
3 What did you disagree with and what would be different in your knowledge map if you agreed with it instead?

YOUR SKILLS OF KNOWING TOOLBAG

4 Why is it important to have a skills of knowing toolbag available in managing knowledge?

5 What would you say if you were asked to discuss with a friend three different ways of knowing?

6 What is one question you can formulate for yourself, which you now want answered having finished this chapter?

7 The expert knowledge manager's top ten tips

Our objectives

- To explore the wider context of using knowledge skills in business.
- To provide a short set of maxims to integrate knowledge skills into your professional practice.
- To describe the common pitfalls of knowledge management and how to avoid them.

'When you wake up in the morning, Pooh,' said Piglet at last, 'what is the first thing you say to yourself?'

'What's for breakfast?' said Pooh. 'What do *you* say, Piglet?'

'I say, I wonder what's going to happen exciting *today*?'

Pooh nodded thoughtfully.

'It's the same thing.'

(A. A. Milne)

How acquiring and understanding are *not* 'the same thing'

Your work experience, and what you know, both tacitly and explicitly, help you turn unrelated facts into expert knowledge, relevant knowledge. Consultants at Arthur Andersen always ask the question 'knowledge to do what?' to help define the context of use. Knowledge for a purpose and within a context of operation is the only useful knowledge, the 'doing the knowing' we talked about in Chapter 2. It is not there to be mined and sold for its intrinsic value like gold. We use this metaphor as a shortcut, but we must remember that knowledge itself is a metaphorical label, a process of knowing that is talked about as if it were a thing or object (see Chapter 6).

Even if, as is the case with knowledge management in business, the context is clear, the purpose may not always be. We can often find the purpose to be surfing the latest fad in management theory which will help managers achieve the holy grail of ever increasing 'efficiency'. In this chapter we give way to this temptation too! We offer a set of shortcuts to help you be more efficient in your knowledge management activities and to develop your knowledge skills. But there is a catch.

The top ten tips will only work if followed in the spirit of lifelong learning: creating knowledge in a cyclic and ongoing way. We know of no tips for accumulating knowledge that will always be relevant and of value; the kind of knowledge we can accumulate as we accumulate magazines and publications 'that we should be reading to keep up to date'. By all means keep those publications. Understanding how and where to find knowledge is key to becoming an expert knowledge manager. We should always be willing to keep acquiring the knowledge that a given situation requires.

An often quoted rationale for knowledge management initiatives is that, as experts leave the organization, we need repositories to store their knowledge so that the organization does not lose the expertise. Organization would do well to be highly suspicious of initiatives that promise this direct transfer of expertise. Since the 1950s, research in artificial intelligence has been looking for the elusive intelligent machine that will perform as an expert might. The search continues today and the answer is unlikely to be in the kind of system that stores knowledge in a static form, no matter how many interesting hyperlinks we are able to create or beautiful networks we can create with our ever fancier interfaces.

Commitment to best management practice requires that we do not become the recipients of recycled technologies that failed to meet the promise of the artificial expert ten years ago. So beware the claims of those, say from the neural networks fraternity, who promise intelligent learning machines without the touch of human hand. At the risk of repeating ourselves, we must stress once more that it is the *combination* of static knowledge representation (such as those reviewed in the next chapter) with individuals who have honed knowledge skills and with networks of knowledge sharing individuals that will create knowledge truly understood, not just merely acquired.

This brings us to the transient nature of value. Knowledge that is of high value today may be useless tomorrow. For example, expert knowledge of sophisticated computer systems which helped one of us get a high first salary, was no longer of value to a career in management development and quickly became outdated in a career as a knowledge engineer. The kind of knowledge needed in the context was of a different nature and it had to be acquired. The skills to acquire new knowledge have been and will continue to be a consistent asset, however. This kind of meta-knowledge has maintained its value throughout our careers.

Our mission in writing this book has been partly to debunk the idea that business success will be determined only by knowledge which can be acquired, validated and stored in big containers, known as computers. Acquisition, storage and validation are not the same as knowledge understanding. They are useful aspects of the process of knowledge working when carried out in conjunction with the creation of networks of people who want to share what they know and individuals who have sophisticated knowledge skills to approach knowledge management as a process of lifelong learning – in other words, when knowledge is available to people who can understand and use it for a purpose.

Nothing is a problem or a discovery in itself, it can be a
problem only if it puzzles somebody, and a discovery only
if it relieves somebody from the burden of a problem.
(Polanyi, 1958)

The top ten tips and more

Here are some tips to help you make the whole of life a
knowledge acquisition adventure, which will allow you to
continue developing as an expert knowledge manager in this
lifelong process of creating knowledge through learning.

Pay attention to what your senses tell you

We explored this tip in detail when we gave you ways of
improving your perceptual literacy. The key to using this tip is
remembering that our perception is highly selective and that
judgements about value are often made just below conscious
awareness. This gets in the way of accurate perception, the
kind of perception that can distinguish between sensory data
and our interpretation of that data. The interpretation will
always be dependent on our models of the world and can, as
such, be limiting. We can in a very real sense not see things as
they are, but as *we* are. The tip we are giving you here is to be
aware of the nature of perception and learn to develop ways to
give yourself time to notice what else is there other than your
immediate judgements about what you see. This will increase
the accuracy of your perception and will, therefore, increase
the choices that are available to you for learning new models
and perspectives that had not formed part of your thinking.

Commit yourself to daily practice

Will everyone then someday practise the meditation
technique taught by the Buddha? Not likely. You may
prefer a different way. But, please find a way. Find a way
that will continually deepen your understanding . . .
(Spretnak, 1993)

Many of the activities that we have included in this book
can be used in an ongoing way to keep refining your skills.

It is an inherent part of a knowledge skill that it can only be developed and nurtured with regular practice. You can read the chapter of a book and create an informal system of categories that describe the knowledge it contains. You can choose to take part of your lunch hour to practise the paying attention activity in Chapter 6. You may choose to take up Alexander technique lessons to free up more energy for your knowledge working. You could choose to acquire a new body of knowledge that is completely divorced from your current context to practise all the skills we have explored with a live example.

Whatever you choose to do, we suggest that you make the commitment to the development of your knowledge skills. They are as much a part of your development possibilities as learning how to use a particular software package. If we cannot manage knowledge we cannot compete in the knowledge society. The focus of this book is less on the organizational side of knowledge management and more on the personal side of it. You have control over yourself and how you develop. Be proactive and make a commitment to using your knowledge skills daily.

Turn work problems into knowledge acquisition projects

You can frame many problems at work (and in your home life) as knowledge management problems. If you assume that every problem has a solution, or more likely many solutions, you can decide what knowledge you need to help you find an appropriate outcome. Think about the kind of knowledge (see Chapter 2) you need to acquire to help you find that solution quickly. Your knowledge skills allow you to go through the whole knowledge management process: from deciding what is to be the knowledge area, to acquiring the data, to creating a framework, to forming a view.

You know what to do and how to do it. Find the knowledge that requires your attention today.

Go beyond words

Learn that there is much more to understanding others in conversation than the content of the words they use. We explored this in depth in Chapter 6 as conversational literacy. There is more to language than the surface level of the words. We can understand the structure of someone else's thinking by learning to listen to the deep level of language. There is much of practical use that we can do to help us do this effectively. Use the tools we gave you and watch your ability to understand others grow. To what end? Having knowledge-bearing conversations in the sense defined in Chapter 3. Going beyond words will help you find the structure of an area of knowledge easily and in much less time than having a conversation without the awareness of what lies behind the words.

Brush up on your metaphor spotting

Our ability to understand the world is fundamentally grounded in the ability to explain one thing in terms of another thing that belongs to a different category. We make sense of our minds in terms of our experiences with our bodies moving in space. Your ability to notice the underlying metaphors of an area of knowledge will give you extremely powerful ways to validate and test knowledge as well as creating new knowledge.

It is as though the ability to comprehend experience through metaphor were a sense, like seeing or touching or hearing. Metaphor is as much part of our functioning as our sense of touch and just as precious. (Lakoff and Johnson, 1980a)

Perhaps, even more importantly, working with metaphor spotting as we suggested in Chapters 5 and 6 can enhance your understanding of what counts as relevant knowledge in your organization. You will then be in a much stronger position to suggest alternative metaphors that may be more aligned with organizational objectives. An important point here is that structuring metaphors evolve unconsciously. We can sometimes act from a metaphor that may be in conflict with stated organizational and personal values. For example, a company may hold integrity as one of its core values. Yet the way in which people behave and interact can point to a structuring metaphor of 'business is war', where the overriding goal is to destroy the competition, viewed as the enemy, by any means available. 'All is fair in love and war', a senior sales executive might be heard saying. This conflict between the metaphor that drives the behaviour and the espoused value will create incongruent behaviour in employees. Your ability to get to this kind of knowledge may serve as the driving force for genuine organizational change.

Know that you already know how . . . in some context

Knowledge skills are learning skills. We know how to learn, though we may have forgotten that it is important for us to continue learning to create new knowledge in adulthood. It is useful to apply this tip when faced with a novel situation, a situation that may, on first meeting, appear to be beyond your current knowledge. Managers face this kind of situation, for example, when they are made redundant at an age where they had assumed lifelong employment. Redundancy counsellors will tell you that the key to supporting these individuals into finding alternative careers is in shifting the belief that what they know is not useful outside their known working environment. Some of the knowledge you need will probably be different, but there will be some components that easily map to new contexts of work. At the very least, you know that you know how to find out what you need. This will reduce your anxiety when faced with new situations.

Reuse what you know

This requires that you think of your knowledge at a high level of abstraction. For example, my knowledge of a particular software package may be outdated, and yet I do know *how to use* a software package. This means that I can learn to use another package that may be more relevant to my current needs. Another example, extensive experience in interviewing experts in car diagnosis and cancer protocols may not be directly relevant to my work in management development. My ability to interview and structure knowledge most certainly is. Reusing what we know requires that we ask: 'How do I use what I know to learn about what I do not know yet?'

Of course you can do it, but do you want to?

This tip speaks to the heart of our organizational lives. Demands on individuals are ever increasing. If you have knowledge assets that your organizations values, professional expertise or an ability to manage others' knowledge, you will get ever increasing requests to contribute your expertise. Your competence is not in question, and you will do well for yourself and for your organization in the long term to constantly ask the above question. A warning: think of *want* in adult terms: Do I want to do this when I think of what my objectives are? How does my doing this contribute to the overall well-being of the organization and, therefore, my well-being? There is a very real and often neglected need for knowledge management efforts to be pursued by people who are personally motivated and highly committed to these efforts. If you really do not want to, for whatever reason, you are unlikely to put in the level of effort that the conscious managing of knowledge requires.

Go for simplicity: do what works!

This one is simple and short: What is the minimum I can do to achieve the result? Clarity of purpose is key. I must know what is the value that my knowledge management activities will add and think about ways to manage more knowledge with less effort. Look at the argument for 'enough thinking' in our final chapter. Practise this tip in conjunction with the next one and you will not only be an expert knowledge manager you will also remain a sane one.

Do not aspire to be a magpie

You must be prepared to go to a meeting and endure comments such as, 'You mean you didn't read *Shortcuts to a Better Casting Project* in the latest *Foundry Lovers News*?' Better to suffer the humiliation of saying you didn't and ask someone else to be kind enough to summarize it, than to have to read all the articles that cross your desk. (Semler, 1993)

A common cause of 'information anxiety', a term coined by Richard Saul Wurman as far back as 1989, is our belief that just because there is knowledge available we must have it at all costs. We do not even have the time to expand the body of knowledge relevant to our professional practice, given the increased rate at which new developments happen. Information superhighways mean that we know the amount of information that is out there and that we do not yet have. If we add to this the perceived need to have knowledge outside our particular discipline to be a more rounded manager, we often find ourselves under immense time pressure to keep up with all the journals and publications to be considered up to date and well informed.

The key to curing this time-illness, as Semler calls it in his excellent book *Maverick* (1993), is to learn to 'be proud of not being aware of everything'. Set yourself an achievable goal that is determined by need rather than greed. Then you will not be seduced into collecting just the superficial, glittering pieces of knowledge in magpie style.

7.1 Now I have got it, what can I do with it

Step 1　*Two of the top ten tips: 'know that you already know how' and 'reuse what you know' emphasize the way that some knowledge is eminently transferable. In this short activity you will look at some of your own areas of knowledge and see how true this is.*

Step 2　*Spend two minutes (more if you find you need it), noting down one-line descriptions of what you are really good at. Maybe the top five or six areas of expertise you have. It can be at work, in your social life . . . anything.*

Step 3　*Now take each of your one-liners. For each think of three other applications of that expertise in a similar, related area.*

Step 4　*Now take each one-liner and think of three other applications in a totally unrelated area. If you cannot think of an appropriate area, think yourself out into the world, looking at what other people are doing. Put your expertise alongside them: see if it could be useful. Be as wild and fanciful as you like in possible application.*

This exercise demonstrates the flexibility of your knowledge – that you are already equipped to deal with many more areas than you thought.

Some common pitfalls in our thinking about knowledge

As we saw in Chapter 2, Brian Woodward (1988) provides a useful framework for knowledge working because he presents a perspective that incorporates even the early stages of the knowledge management process. His goal is to produce expert computer systems, but the approach remains relevant to our interests. To review briefly, he characterized the knowledge acquisition process as having three phases: phase 1, understanding the knowledge area; phase 2, the detailed iterative process of acquiring knowledge, which includes the implementation of a knowledge base; phase 3, the installation and maintenance phase. Most knowledge management efforts are geared towards phase 2 activity and this means that certain decisions about the knowledge area have already been made in an unsystematic way.

At some point, the domain is defined before the application of specific knowledge acquisition techniques.
(Woodward, 1988)

It is paying attention to phase 1 that leads us into noticing some common pitfalls. These pitfalls highlight common mistaken assumptions that we can make about the process of working with knowledge. We note them below to help you avoid them in the future. We urge you to notice and challenge fellow knowledge workers when they fall into any of the pits below!

Pitfall 1: the decision on what is appropriate knowledge is a top-down process

Falling into this pitfall, you look for the kind of data that will fit your existing models; you look for the knowledge structures you currently use. If you know that your particular requirement will need a certain type of knowledge with specific parameters, you ask: where in my current sphere of experience can I find such knowledge? Sometimes this will work. Often, though, you will miss very useful data because you will not have known what it was that you did not know!

With a strongly structured area of knowledge, your process becomes a matter of 'simply' specifying a particular instance of a given top-down model.

For example, you know about marketing a car to the public, so you treat a group of automotive journalists whose opinions you are supposed to be eliciting to an hour of marketing speak. Result – these experts feel thoroughly patronized and say terrible things about your car. Alternatively, you may characterize the nature of the knowledge area in terms of more generic knowledge types, such as this is a diagnosis, planning or a classification type of problem. So you try to force the area you are trying to find out about on to a map what you already know.

This solution can work very well when phase 1 activity has been completed; that is, if you already know what kind of knowledge you are looking for, you can use what you know already to help you get started. Be aware however, that you are making certain assumptions about the nature of the data that is the input to the process, and on the characteristics of the acquisition process, and that they may be inaccurate. There may be times when a bottom-up approach, one where you suspend assumptions, bracketing your theories and preconceptions, may yield higher quality knowledge.

Pitfall 2: having equivalent knowledge is enough to replace expertise

Knowledge management initiatives are about finding ways to represent tacit and explicit knowledge in ways that are somehow equivalent to the knowledge experts possess. Please note that we said 'equivalent'. This is to be clearly distinguished from being able to exactly duplicate the results that an expert would be produce. When we talk about storing and exploiting the knowledge for the organization once the expert has been made redundant or has left we are confusing something equivalent with something identical. The static knowledge in a computer is useful with humans who understand it around; it is less than worthless without them. We still do not understand enough about the human mind to be able to say that we can extract the kind of knowledge that would allow us to say that a system 'contains' the expert's knowledge. It may contain a useful representation of the knowledge which can then be used as the basis for developing greater expertise in human knowledge sources, but that is the most that managing knowledge can promise. Current computer systems are mainly repositories of static knowledge. Only expert systems have a mechanism to do some basic 'thinking', and this is nothing like the thinking that humans are capable of. Extensive hyperlinks are very helpful for humans wanting to make sense of masses of information, but they are not 'sense-making' tools! We must keep checking what specifically are we capturing when we acquire knowledge?

Pitfall 3: representing knowledge is just a matter of identifying known structures

The issue here is about deciding on what is relevant enough. How we approach this problem very much depends on our perceptions of the nature of the data we want to acquire. If the data is quantitative, we just need to identify the variables of interest and work with those. Rarely is the kind of knowledge we want to obtain in business of this kind; it is often the messy knowledge which humans hold in subsidiary awareness that permits them to perform as expert in their fields. It is this that makes the knowledge valuable. The data that is input to the process, therefore, tends to be qualitative. This means that we must derive theoretical constructs, like metaphors, from messy linguistic data. How we initially represent the data is often left unspecified, and with this the process that decides if it is relevant. Clarity about this issue will stop you from having unrealistic expectations about what you will be able to do with the knowledge and, more importantly, will ensure that you consideration of 'the knowledge to do what?' the priority it deserves. The quality of your output will be dependent on how systematically you approach this stage.

Pitfall 4: acquiring knowledge is purely an analytic activity

There is a perception that only an analytic process is involved in managing knowledge effectively. Expert system research has clearly demonstrated that the process entails both analysis and synthesis. Through analysis, knowledge that exists 'out there', independent of knowledge sources, can be *found*. Through synthesis new knowledge is *created* that makes sense of the input data, perhaps through the development of a model or theory that did not exist before.

The initial stage where we determine the boundaries of the area of knowledge to be worked on is very much a synthetic activity. Synthesis can create a problem for knowledge managers because in trying to 'capture expertise' it is counter-intuitive to accept the notion of the creation of an entity that did not exist before capture. Envisaged problems with validity and testing help us create the illusion that analysis will deliver everything. If we buy into this pitfall the quality of our knowledge will suffer.

Pitfall 5: knowledge management occurs in a vacuum

Knowledge management activities are often assumed to occur in a vacuum. Knowledge is acquired from a knowledge source; often the knowledge source itself determines what is valid knowledge; once captured the knowledge can be stored and once stored it can be leveraged. Although this approach may be appropriate when dealing with areas that allow a straightforward mapping of reality onto our representation, it clouds important structuring processes when dealing with more complex topics. And almost by definition, knowledge management initiatives rarely deal with simple matters. The role of human beings in the process of making knowledge explicit for public consumption is crucial to initial under-standing of the knowledge area. Human beings determine what is worth gathering. The assumption that knowledge can 'exist' in a vacuum, has led to the creation of metaphors such a mining knowledge assets (Leonard, 1997) to refer to the human process of conversation that is the very essence of any knowledge management activity. Whilst making it easier to talk about knowledge, this assumption can lead us into dehumanizing knowledge work.

Knowledge acquisition is more than just the 'transfer of expertise'. Knowledge acquisition is a creative process in which systems builders construct qualitative models of human behaviour. (Musen, 1988)

Understand these pitfalls as they apply to your initial attempts to define the knowledge to be acquired or captured, and you will find yourself managing the kind of knowledge that has value and can be truly supportive of your knowledge intensive activities.

Summary

We have come a long way. From Winnie the Pooh to the distinctions between synthesis and analysis! We started this chapter with an exploration of the differences that there are between acquiring knowledge and understanding knowledge. The kind of knowledge that is supportive of your knowledge activities is the kind that is understood within a context for a purpose, and not the kind that exists as inert matter in some kind of knowledge heaven. We strongly suggested that value is relative and ever changing, and that the constant is in our willingness and skill to keep acquiring new knowledge. Within that context we discussed tips to help you with this process of turning unrelated facts into expert knowledge through experience. We ended the chapter with a set of common pitfalls which people who work in the knowledge business can easily fall into. These encouraged you to see knowledge management as inherently qualitative and embedded in human interaction.

Learning review

Some questions to help you review your learning from this chapter might be:

1 If you were to tell a colleague about this chapter what would you say?
2 What is the one nugget that you may find yourself quoting over coffee?
3 What did you find most useful in this chapter?
4 Why is it useful to be willing to always acquire new knowledge?
5 What would you say if you were asked to discuss with a friend the most common pitfalls in knowledge management?
6 What is one question you can formulate for yourself, which you want to reflect on as you read the next chapter?

8 Knowledge skills and information technology

Our objectives

- To make explicit links between knowledge skills and the technological and organizational aspects of knowledge management.
- To provide you with an overview of other aspects of knowledge management and resources for finding out more.
- To argue that knowledge management must be grounded in people and that the success of knowledge management initiatives is dependent on individuals developing the skills presented in this book.

You and the knowledge management revolution . . . or evolution?

It is impossible to explore knowledge skills without mentioning information technology (IT). We have become quite used to being told that technology will solve our problems and those developing IT knowledge management tools are already well down the road to success. Later in the chapter you will see a number of products and initiatives, heavily dependent on information technology. It is only a matter of time before these idiosyncratic systems coalesce, fragment and splinter into a range of highly marketable products. This knowledge management industry is part of a general technology-driven evolution where the existence of a technical solution creates a market for itself. So having the ability to store and retrieve large amounts of data drives companies into wanting to store and retrieve large amounts of data.

Added to this is the maxim 'knowledge is a corporate asset' or 'knowledge is intellectual capital', which leads us into developing ways of preserving and measuring this asset for competitive advantage. We suggest that the knowledge management revolution is not a new phenomenon. In fact it seems more of a natural evolution for doing business in the West. We understand capital and it is, therefore, natural to think of knowledge as intellectual capital. However, as we said in Chapter 2, the early development of knowledge management has been hijacked by information technologists who have reduced the knowledge management problem to one of representing company knowledge in a company knowledge archive. Our plea is to recognize that while the technology is essential for effective knowledge management, it is not sufficient. The essentially human skills are still needed and may even be impeded by the dominance of the software.

What can technology do for you?

Technology is often better used as a connector for knowledge rather than a capturer. (Laurence Prusak, IBM Consulting Group)

The technology being developed in this area is changing so rapidly that it is a daily job to keep abreast of the shifts.

Technology can help to:

- support thinking and decisions
- provide access to information through structured storage
- interpret data
- disseminate information
- facilitate the emergence of cross-functional teams.

In the next section we will look at examples of each of these applications. For more detail, see Appendix 4 which covers a much wider range of products and technologies.

Supporting thinking and decisions

While software is not capable of creative thought in itself, it can support thinking and decision-making by pulling appropriate information together, evaluating and providing guidance based on knowledge which has been modelled in an expert system.

Arthur Andersen

Consultants Arthur Andersen use both pure information systems and those which can more actively support decision-making. They typify the difference in this way:

Convergent systems	Divergent systems
● Codified information	● Not extensively codified
● Top down	● Bottom up
● All information verified	● Not all verified
● Periodically updated	● Real-time input/debate
● Historical information	● Innovative/work in progress
● Disseminating	● Creating
● Classification	● Fluid categories
● Not group centric	● Group centric
● Information extracted from field	● Information offered by field

Accessing information through structured storage

There are many ways of storing information with some associated structure. Although not the most sophisticated, the hypertext approach used by the Internet's World Wide Web has become such a standard that its familiarity and extensive support make it a more effective pragmatic solution than more heavy duty structured storage.

Technology: intranet

An intranet is an internal company network using exactly the same technology as the Internet's World Wide Web. This has proved a very effective means of providing structured information, as the tools to generate and manage the environment are very highly developed (and cheap), and the compatibility with the web means that it is possible to seamlessly link out to relevant external information from anywhere in the world.

Buckman Laboratories

Buckman Laboratories developed K'Netix – an intranet which connects all employees, particularly associates who were working in different parts of the world, to knowledge resources and contacts. The driving force was to increase customer contact and a Vice-President of Knowledge Transfer was appointed in 1991. K'Netix allows access to experts and library resources, problem-solving groups, unrestricted communication across geographical locations. Benefits include speed of response to customers and improved creativity of new products.

Interpreting data

Data alone is effectively worthless. Information technology systems can distribute and even generate interpretations that turn the data into the sort of information which can support the building of knowledge.

Technology: Executive Information System

The Executive Information System (EIS) is a classic example of data interpretation. Such systems take feeds from a wide range of company data sources, then combine and interpret the outputs to produce a concise summary and key performance indicators for the company. Usually an EIS will provide facilities to 'drill down' into the data to expand on a particular part of the information.

Allied Domecq

Allied Domecq use a wide range of technology to support knowledge work, including:

- competitive databases
- project tracking system
- project development database
- EIS for tracking movements towards destination
- MIS for looking at knowledge and information
- consumer research system.

Disseminating information

There is a subtle distinction between structured storage of information, which is essentially passive, waiting to be read, and disseminating information, which is more active, bringing the information to the attention of the recipient, though both fall within the same spectrum of systems.

Technology: intranet

See above.

ICL

ICL's Café VIK set up as a web site on ICL's intranet with a friendly design using a cartoon character. Business benefits identified by ICL are being able to contact client managers quickly, greater awareness of customer issues and opportunities, and specialists can access 'technology watch' for latest briefings.

Facilitating the emergence of cross-functional teams

As business throws off the shackles of the production line, the cross-functional team, bringing in expertise from different parts of the company, has come into its own. Technology can help such teams, especially when physically dispersed, to work more effectively together. Some make it easier for remote teams to work better in real time, such as network-based meeting products that can provide anything from electronic whiteboards to video conferencing. Others act more like a massive, structured team bulletin board.

Technology: Lotus Notes

Lotus Notes is a document database which offers different views of databases, e.g. by process, industry, company, topic, performance measure. It can be thought of as envelopes which take a variety of items and assists in workflow and automated business processes. Its great advantage is the ability to replicate so that remote stations can work on and change a document, sharing knowledge and using brainstorming techniques. Its search facility is also a powerful tool, e.g. for providing a complete customer profile from existing knowledge. It resembles Windows Explorer and contains applications such as databases, discussion threads. There is also a NotesBench Consortium Web site run by an independent organization dedicated to providing Domino and Notes performance information to customers. There are 20 million Notes users world-wide. Other software systems can be built on top of Lotus Notes, e.g. 'Knowledge Express' of American Management Systems.

British Airways

British Airways uses Lotus Notes for a variety of learning and change processes. The Change Forum is an application allowing requests for changes, e.g. putting on a larger aircraft for a particularly heavy load. All requests are posted and every stakeholder (e.g. marketing, scheduling, crewing, etc.) in the process is able to see the stage the request is at. Each party is able to comment on difficulties and accept or reject the request. Once all parties have given the go ahead the change is made. As it is now an easier process rather than the previous tedious method of sending telexes, more changes are made with increased profits.

The Mods Forum is another application with a built in e-mail so that responses can be prompted. It is used for technical adjustments to aircraft and has a built-in analysis function which calculates cost and work involved. Pilots' flight reports can be accessed and used as a learning tool where similar incidents have happened before rather than filed.

What might be your first step?

As one of our researchers said: 'This is such a huge area, where do you start? It has taken me days to just begin to understand the jargon.' Those of you new to this area may well share her feeling once you start looking at some of the resources in the appendices. Our researcher was particularly frustrated by the tendency of resources to talk about knowledge management rather than about the how of managing knowledge. She came to us one day with a pained expression on her face and said: 'If I hear the word leverage one more time . . . but just how do you do it?'

A consultant, working at a top consultancy firm which specializes in knowledge management and uses internal knowledge networks for knowledge sharing within a comprehensive knowledge management initiative, came to us to discuss some of the assumptions of the initiative. He said: 'What are knowledge objects and what do they do? Everyone is very concerned with best practice and putting "it" into the system and when I ask, Who defines best practice? And how do you know it is best practice? These questions get lost in the eagerness to capture "it" and store "it", whatever the "it" is.' He was puzzled by the way in which highly intelligent people seem to lose their critical thinking abilities when faced with the illusion of creating 'knowledge objects' which can be treated as fact once they have the particular structure a computer system requires. Irrespective of the quality of the data that was used for its creation. This is a common problem in the development of expert systems. A very hard problem indeed.

In the experience of our researcher and the consultant lies the ground for your first step – and possibly for many subsequent steps too!

Notice within yourself the way you choose to think about the use of technology. You may be making assumptions about the credibility of an approach on the basis of the numbers of words you do not understand. The argument might run something like this: 'The greater number of words I do not understand the more likely this is to be the approach I need.' If you allow this assumption to go unchallenged in your own thinking you will spend, or more accurately waste, a great deal of time learning jargon to get to the essence of what it can actually do for you.

There may be many other assumptions you are making that you must challenge to allow yourself to start asking the kind of questions that our two stories demonstrate. The knowledge management field, due to its close connections with technology, is full of nominalizations (long words that need reconnecting back to experience – like nominalization) and often incompetence hides behind these. To sort out that which is of value and that which is not, you must challenge the assumptions that stop you from thinking critically and ask penetrating questions of the data that is being presented to you as knowledge. Remember that it is not knowledge until it is of value to you. If it can be explained and connected to your experience, and it addresses an issue you and your organization have, then you may choose to take it on board. Your task is to understand, not to learn a foreign language that belongs to a country you may never travel to.

Some questions suggested by Joanna Howard (1998) to help this critiquing process are:

- Who is this person anyway? Locate the person who presents the approach and understand their background.
- What was going on at the time? Understand the history, the context and the basic assumptions that may explain the content. For example, knowledge management is firmly rooted in technology and this root will give it a particular bias as regards its values.

- In what way is that similar to now? This will help you understand the extent of the match between their context and the reality you have to deal with daily. You may need to include certain things that the approach leaves out or vice versa.
- What happens when this approach is actually applied? Your task here is to honestly look for real-life outcomes, actively seek that which is positive, that which is negative and that which may simply be interesting.
- Why do I like or dislike it? This question is often ignored. You will gain a lot of useful information if you can articulate and understand what you might label your gut feel or intuition. Remember all that was said about intuition in Chapter 6.

 If perception samples experience *only* in order to categorize it, and to decide whether it is potentially useful or harmful, the conscious image it creates is likely to be rather flat and dull. (Guy Claxton, 1997)

Finally, we suggest that as your first step you could do worse than to do a little 'apply to self'. You can use all the skills we have worked on in this book to understand knowledge management itself. Knowledge management initiatives often lack a clear scope. The area to be covered is implicitly defined as the business processes and know-how needed to achieve organizational objectives. For example, a mission statement from a knowledge management team within a large corporation might read: 'That we know what we know, learn what we need to learn, and use our knowledge more productively than any other company'. The level of generality in such a statement begs for a tighter definition. If the subject is business knowledge, what is the nature of that knowledge? It may be the type of knowledge that cannot be made explicit – perhaps the organization can never know what it knows. Cognitive science is full of distinctions for different knowledge types and analyses of the feasibility of bringing certain types of knowledge into consciousness. We referred to this in Chapter 2 and we will say more in our concluding remarks. In sum, you must start and continue to question the quality of the data that is input to knowledge management initiatives. Capital letters may create the illusion of a Knowledge Object, but do not a valid knowledge object make!

8.1 Word watch

Step 1   *Obtain a catalogue of technical products in an area you do not understand (ideally from a retailer who stocks several different brands). Find a particularly juicy type of product – say video projectors or lawn mowers or defibrillators. Read through the descriptions of the competing products. Decide which you think is best, ignoring price.*

Step 2   *Now look again at the catalogue. What elements of the description persuaded you that one was better than another (bearing in mind you know nothing about this product)? This can be a good example of the way information technology can seduce the knowledge manager into a knee-jerk reaction that they need software to solve their problem. 'It's a knowledge-based problem, so we need Notes' (or whatever). Do not be distracted by the lure of technology. Bring it in to meet a need, not to wear the right designer label.*

Summary

- We explore here the links that between your knowledge skills and knowledge management.
- We remind you that information technology is essential for getting your knowledge management initiative up and running, but the individual applying their skills so deftly is even more important.
- The technology being developed in this area is changing so rapidly that it is a daily job to keep abreast of the shifts. We give you some ways of categorizing the type of technology that is available and have explored what to think about when considering your first step.

Learning review

Some questions to help you review your learning from this chapter might be:

1 If you were to tell a colleague about this chapter what would you say?
2 What is the one nugget that you may find yourself quoting over coffee?
3 What did you disagree with and what would be different in your knowledge map if you agreed with it instead?
4 What would you say if you were asked to discuss with a friend three different ways in which technology can support you in managing knowledge?
5 What is one question you can formulate for yourself, which you now want answered having finished this chapter?

Learning review

9 Knowledge and the future

Enlightened knowledge management initiatives work by bringing together structures to support knowledge sharing, such as virtual team work and peer assistance, with the development of abilities in people, such as improving their communication skills to allow them to be effective at sharing knowledge. Technology-based support is provided where appropriate, but with consideration for people and company culture issues.

An aspect worth highlighting here is time. An organization that is serious about enhancing its knowledge management abilities, needs to put the systems in place that allow individuals to do more than pay lip service to the process. If knowledge management and the development of the necessary skills are to be more than a passing fad, organizations will have to put their money where their mouth is – in this case, by making fewer demands of their managers and other employees in order to free them up to engage in knowledge management with colleagues.

It is difficult to do, even when the need is recognized. Some companies, such as British Airways, are building new headquarters sites with huge open meeting spaces, specifically designed for knowledge sharing. Yet there needs to be a further step – to allow a proportion of the staff's time to actually perform this task. You only have to look at all the reports on how much employee time is 'wasted' using e-mail and surfing the net. By implication, if the staff do not have their noses to the grindstone, they are not working. Certainly they may be wasting time, but there is no recognition of the need to spend time building knowledge.

... but the emphasis on profits and the maximization of shareholder value ignores the two most significant forces acting on companies today: The shift to knowledge as the critical production factor and the changing world environment. (de Geus, 1997)

It will take time and practise to hone your knowledge skills. If you are to feel that the effort is worth it, you have to be rewarded for this. Performance management systems can become a paper-shuffling exercise in which the spirit of the system is lost to the excessive time demands made on managers. The forms are hurriedly filled in to comply with the systems, but the coaching and feedback skills that are supposed to make the systems effective take second place to the achievement of more immediate business objectives.

Filling in the forms without attention to quality and usefulness could lead to large repositories of unmanageable and meaningless data. We could find ourselves acquiring anything under the guise of valuable knowledge because individuals and teams do not have the dedicated time to give the initiative the time and attention that is needed to produce high-quality knowledge. As we saw in Chapter 8, the process of managing knowledge is not purely a matter of transferring knowledge assets resident in people to a computer system. The process requires that we determine what the organization finds of relevance and value, and that it allows groups to work together with high levels of knowledge skills to take part in communication processes to generate valuable knowledge.

The potential pitfall of acquiring meaningless data can only be avoided if an organization sees knowledge management as part of its day-to-day business life; if knowledge management activities are given as much value and time as other business objectives. There is no shortcut to this. Everything in this book will help individuals become expert knowledge managers, but the organization has to do more than think of this initiative as an interesting add-on that will not use up time resources from their key people. We must remember that knowledge assets worth preserving are often key people in the organization. Does the long-term organizational strategy allow for people to deliver clear performance targets around the use of their knowledge management skills? This question cannot be underestimated. We pose it here in our final chapter because, though not our main focus, a positive answer to it is a prerequisite for any successful initiative that will allow you and your staff to use your knowledge skills in the service of organizational change.

Getting your organization down the knowledge-sharing route

Applying what you have learned to the reality of your day-to-day deserves some attention given our comments above. We approach this issue from the basis of value. Part of your honed skills has to include an ability to spot opportunities for small steps in the direction of a knowledge-aware culture in the organization. It may be that, having read this book, you are to be a pioneer in your organization. Here are some questions to ask yourself:

- If there were one problem that, if it were solved, would make those you report to sleep like a baby, what would it be?
- Ask the same question applied to yourself
- What aspect of that solution is knowledge dependent?
- What is the high-leverage knowledge that is needed?
- Who or what has the expertise?
- How much time can I realistically free up to take on this project?
- What do I need to do to get buy-in for the project?
- What value will it add?
- What will be my output (e.g. networks of relationships, a model of the knowledge, pointers to people who have the expertise and are willing to share it, you will gain the expertise and be able to use to solve the problem)?
- How will I make the knowledge available to others (e.g. meeting of virtual teams, knowledge-sharing groups around the theme, a technology-based system)?

A serious look at these questions will help you select a first project that is likely to be high profile and of high value to your organization. We suggest that this the most useful first step you could take to bring knowledge into your organization's agenda.

A memo to your manager on the subject of 'how we should change things around here' can be a useful output, if you can make clear recommendations on the basis of the results of your project. Effective use of your company's knowledge assets indicates that a company can be flexible and can more easily adapt to the changing environment. As such it is a huge competitive advantage. This may help you get your organization interested. Establishing a culture that takes people, processes and technology as partners to the creation of a knowledge sharing culture is a long-term goal which needs backing.

The ability to learn faster than your competitors, may be the only sustainable competitive advantage. (de Geus)

People focused on short-term gains will not see the significance of managing knowledge effectively. It requires investment of time and financial resources for little immediate payback. It requires that managers understand that the shift to a knowledge society, as Arie de Geus (1997) describes it in his book *The Living Company*, is here to stay and is at odds with a model of organizations that uses the machine as a metaphor for its structure. If we see the company as a machine for making money, we will behave very differently than we would if we saw it as a living being. If longevity of the organization is a goal that is chosen in favour of short-term maximization of profit with minimization of resources, then we have no choice but to invest in people. Profitability becomes a means to the end of longevity. The behaviours that support the creation of knowledge companies are in line with the skills that we have explored in this book.

Perhaps a key question to ask before embarking on getting commitment from your organization to managing knowledge might be 'has this organization chosen to be an economic company or a living company?' An honest answer to this question may well save you a lot of wasted effort and might lead instead to seeking ways in which the underlying metaphor can change . . . or to find an organization where there is already a dawning that survival means effective knowledge management, and that it is people learning together to continue creating knowledge that will give organizations a sustainable advantage. The effective use of knowledge generates organizational expertise, human capital, which may be the only in-road to real organizational change.

From a learning orientation the nurturing of people and the nurturing of capital reinforce each other. (de Geus, 1997)

Learning is our ability to adapt to our environment. Piaget refers to this type of learning as 'learning by accommodation'. Even if you are working in the context of an economic company, as is most likely, you can use the knowledge skills we have explored in this book to develop your own knowledge assets. It will make you more marketable in the knowledge society and will give you greater control over your future: You know that you can acquire the knowledge that the changing world requires from you. And this may be your most important asset in the long term. Organizations are rethinking their measures of long-term success, according to de Geus. Measure your success in terms of your knowledge skills.

A key guiding principle of this book has been to provide support for busy managers and professionals who need to learn about new management skills, of which knowledge skills are but one. We have argued for the use of highly honed skills, rather than for the search of the Holy Grail of the latest piece of software or the latest information management tool, with its inevitable steep learning curve. In sum, we have argued that less is more and that effective knowledge management is about smart use of analytical and tacit skills; the pursuit of more knowledge irrespective of purpose will not lead to success. To be expert knowledge managers we must constantly ask: Have I got *enough* knowledge to achieve my goal?

KNOWLEDGE AND THE FUTURE

On why 'more thinking' does not work anymore

Since the advent of the industrial age we have had a terrific word: MORE. It really worked for everything. When our roads became crowded, we built more roads. When our cities became unsafe, we hire more police officers, ordered more police cars, and built more prisons. (Wurman, 1989)

We tend to apply 'more thinking' to managing knowledge. If we have a problem we just acquire more knowledge. The more we know the richer we are in intellectual assets. Using the economic company model, it follows that we must continue to grow. We must double our intellectual capital from year to year, or so the metaphor directs our behaviour. There is one problem to this way of thinking. We are running out of time to acquire more knowledge at the same time as we acquire more money and at the same time as we acquire more wives or husbands or children, more houses and more cars.

As the economy turns faster, with job-turnovers, 24-hour markets, high-speed transport, fast food, kitchen appliances, we lose rather than gain time to do what really counts. (Ed Mayo, 1997)

Knowledge is changing so rapidly today that even those in full-time education have trouble keeping up with the latest research. A university lecturer at Caltech, a highly prestigious academic institution in California, said, 'it takes all the hours in the day and night to just keep up with what I need to know about my subject area. I just cannot find the time to get ahead and generate new knowledge'. It is relevant to this story that this person is working in a highly specialized area of technology and that he does not have to consider breadth of knowledge but depth. His area of expertise is very specific and yet he is running out of time. The amount he has to know in order to make new discoveries is itself a limit to the growth and advance of technology.

As managers we wait and expect that technological innovations will continue at the speed we have become used to in the last twenty years. We will get the machine that will, at last, allow us to stop and ask where our lives have gone. Technological advance is slowing down; we are not making the leaps we need in order to address the quality of life issues we are facing in our management careers. The unlimited capacity machine will not arrive to save us from the information overload we are experiencing. If the answer does not lie in more computing capacity, then more what?

Oh, yes! The answer must be more training and development. Turn people into unlimited capacity machines. This may sound harsh and yet you need only witness the huge growth in the training and development market for some evidence of this trend. The promise management development professionals make is also of a 'more -ish' nature – more effective managers, staff that can do more with less, more profits, more balance in life, and let us not forget more knowledge and skills to make even more money. We have courses on accelerated learning and brain-based learning where you learn to use more of your brain, rapid reading where you learn to read many more pages per minute.

Clever mental techniques miss the point if they leave in place the same questing, restless attitude of mind. Instead of calling a meeting to 'discuss' the problem, you call one to 'brainstorm' it, or to get people to draw it with crayons. But the pressure for results, the underlying impatience is still there. (Guy Claxton, 1997)

Training and development has a purpose and can genuinely help people manage their jobs better. We have explored in this book a set of skills that will help you manage knowledge *more effectively.* The point we are making is that neither the technology nor the training will continue increasing capacity in an unlimited way. We may be reaching a point where 'more thinking' will not work for us anymore. A point where the hare, to use Guy Claxton's (1997) metaphor, may well have had 'a run for its money' in our world.

More thinking may well lead us to an error message in our mind that reads: 'C:> Fatal system error. Please reboot the machine' – only we do not know how to plug ourselves back in yet. We are running a serious risk of dying from a new disease called information-overload syndrome and yet we need to hold more and more in order to work with complex machines and global organizations.

The answer lies partly in skill development and partly in technology. But more crucially it lies, we believe, in our willingness to change our attitude. When thinking about knowledge we must move to 'enough thinking'. The question shifts from 'How can I acquire more knowledge?' to 'Do I have enough knowledge to get the result?' With this change, our knowledge management skills can be used in a sustainable way to know what we need to know and to let go of the impossible dream of knowing it all, the dream that is so often implied but seldom spoken of in our quest for effective knowledge management.

In practising 'enough thinking' we may be doing more than managing knowledge. A consumption-dependent mindset may not be conducive to our individual longevity, let alone to the longevity of the organizations we work in. This skill may also help our organizations to shift their underlying metaphor towards that of a 'living company' thus helping the creation of new models for the organizations of the future. Downshifting (Ghazi and Jones, 1997) and disorganization (Clegg and Birch, 1998) show an emerging trend that may be indicative that as a society we are becoming aware of the limitations of 'more thinking'.

The second clear message is that people and their attitude to sharing knowledge are central to creating it and using it for competitive advantage and creating profit. (Peter Murray and Andrew Myers, Cranfield School of Management)

Knowledge management is designed to support and enhance the human communication and knowledge-sharing processes. It can be thought of as a team-enabling technology. For example, the Xerox Palo Alto Research Center stimulates innovation by grouping unlikely combinations of professionals (anthropologists, artists, computer scientists). As such it requires that a strong and open team communications and knowledge-sharing culture be developed, and supported by a coaching and facilitative management style. Managing knowledge can be done in the spirit of trust, open communication, learning and sharing. 'Enough thinking' can be brought into initiatives and, we believe, it must if the approach is to become any more than a passing fad. There is no substitute for addressing people management issues and this is our rationale for dedicating this book to the personal skills you need to find your way in the knowledge society.

Knowledge finds its ultimate expression in the decision-making process, and yet on this key subject there is very little information to be found. (de Geus, 1997)

Knowledge, knowing and learning: a lifelong cycle

European Business thinks knowledge is hot and valuable – but still are not prepared to reward their staff for creating sharing or exploiting it. (*Information Strategy*, September 1997)

Locate it, store it, transfer it and retrieve it. First you must acquire it. Where is it? 'Inside people's heads'. Traditional knowledge acquisition for expert systems shows that even for simple problems, it is unwise to ignore the human component of the system. The framework we have presented here acknowledges the importance of all the components of the system.

Emergent knowledge is key for the future of our organizations. Where is the knowledge? We can say that it is distributed in the conversations and informal stories told by those who belong to an organization in the traditional sense, or to a network of people linked by common interests. We would do well to always treat knowledge as having only relative value and as being highly dependent on the context in which it occurs for keeping its value. When we talk of assessing and measuring knowledge as if it had absolute value we run the risk of forgetting that taken out of context, my highly valuable knowledge may be worthless. The greatest asset we have as human beings is our ability to apply the process of learning to new events. I may know how to get what I want from my chief executive and that is valuable knowledge. When he or she is replaced by somebody else, it is my skill at acquiring new and relevant knowledge about this new person that will serve the same purpose as the old knowledge.

We find it difficult to accept that knowledge is not actually money. We have a dream that through accumulating knowledge we may become wise in our old age. Bateson (1997) says that 'wisdom is having the experience of having been wrong so many times, that we are still open to learning' and that definitely comes with age. We can accumulate ways of knowing and skill, knowledge will continue to change and become obsolete at an astounding rate and we will never know it all. Let us not transfer our consumer society mindset to knowledge. We will not end up millionaires in knowledge – we would end up hanging on to a lot of old coins that would weigh a lot and be worth nothing. Technology allows us to store and access much, much more than we can in our head. The argument holds even more in connection with computers; the knowledge 'it' holds is only as valuable as it is useful to the human beings who access it to achieve a particular purpose. This is a clear situation where quantity is most definitely not quality.

Computers are useless, they can only give you answers.
(Pablo Picasso)

Knowledge management initiatives can uncover knowledge and store it as a model of best practice. We must challenge ourselves to keep asking: 'Best practice according to whom?' Once stored in a computer system, what may have been an approximation of very limited application could easily take on the mantle of 'fact'. Human beings will find meaning in the most arbitrary of signs and symbols. This is extremely relevant to our knowledge management endeavours, for we must be careful not to lose sight of just how arbitrary and context-dependent our notions of best practice can be.

People have begun to think of themselves as objects able to fit into the inflexible calculations of disembodied machines: Machines for which the human form-of-life must be analysed into meaningless facts, rather than a *field of concern organized by sensory-motor skills*. Our risk is not the advent of super-intelligent computers, but of sub-intelligent human beings. (Hubert L. Dreyfus, 1992)

Initiatives that continue to combine people, process and technology, without hidden assumptions that the technology will outperform the human, stand a higher chance of success. In organizational life we are not pursuing the goal of creating superintelligent computers. Most initiatives are about connecting people to enable knowledge creation and sharing, combined with a desire to understand what we know, to be able to measure it and exploit it. It is this desire that we believe is misguided. In divorcing knowledge from people we become able to talk about exploitation and control. Only people using and honing their knowledge management skills can bring knowledge to life in situations where the work consists of 'a swampy lowland where situations are confusing messes incapable of a technical solution' (Schon, 1988) – this is the reality of the new millennium organizations. Knowledge is not an object to be exploited and controlled, and it will never become one. It is ever-changing and embodied in people who are constantly creating spheres of knowledge for new purposes through learning from experience in a lifelong cycle. If we need a metaphor to talk about knowledge, perhaps a more sustainable one would be that of knowledge as an organism. This would help us think of knowledge as nothing more than knowing in action. This book has introduced the skills of knowing – now it is time for you to put them into action.

KNOWLEDGE AND THE FUTURE

Appendix 1: Conversational literacy in action

Chapters 5 and 6 describe a set of skills which expert knowledge managers can use when determining what is relevant in a new subject area. We now present some segments of an interview with a Deputy Head of a London School (SA). Our comments are in square brackets and the linguistic expressions being targeted are in italics. The interviewer (I) uses the toolbag presented in Chapter 6.

SA: It depends on the outcomes I want. The topics are less important than *getting* the learning outcomes. I know the children, so I know what I want to get to *build* what I want.

I: What are the basic principles you follow?

SA: You have to make sure that the topics *challenge* the pupils, you are after *expanding limits*, *pushing out* what the kid can do, *breaking down walls* ... [Challenge: referring to an action or process as if it were an object or thing. Sense (feel) language: expanding limits, pushing out, breaking down walls.]

I: So *challenge* has to be *built in*, [from the previous response: Sense (feel) language] and in planning you have to make sure that *what you cover breaks down walls*, and that is an important aspect how you decide what goes where on that blackboard you mentioned earlier. Tell me of an experience in your past that taught the importance of this. [accessing sensory based language, through the expert's past experience. A story that is an example of this follows. Deleted.]

I: And how was that experience important? [A question which can start to search for structure in the subject area.]

SA: That taught me the importance of designing a task in a way that involved the child. I know how to do that because I have been doing it for many years and I know my kids, the topics will be provided by the National Curriculum and that is not the most important thing. It is how you approach it which allows them to keep interested and *push out barriers*. [A statement about knowing how to do the planning task, without knowing explicitly. 'Pushing out barriers', a sense (feel) term was targeted.]

I: You use words like: build, push out, expand, break down walls. Is the image you have one of a building? Are you constructing a building? [A direct question about the metaphor being used, based on the access points targeted earlier.]

SA: No. it's a wall. a wall is the barrier which stops the child learning [The guess made by the interviewer about the image is corrected. What he sees is a wall and volunteers what it means.]

I: So where is the wall? How do you see that? [Exploring the properties of the image: location of the wall image. The emphasis is shifted away from the content of the response and we start exploring the structure or process: How do you see the wall?]

SA: Here is the child (picks up a pen and draws) and here is the wall (all around the child). The wall stops them from seeing what there is beyond. [Having obtained the first image, the expert explains how he is representing the structure.]

I: So what is your role in this picture? [Continue to explore the image. If the child is surrounded by a wall, where are you? Location property of the image.]

SA: My role is to recognize *the wall*, give the child the means with which to *break through*. It's like I plan the lessons in a way that starts *loosening the bricks*, if I'm successful maybe the child can get to see other possibilities that he had not considered. So in planning I need to think about how to make the *wall vulnerable, undermine its foundations*!

[This is a list of the words that were noted down during the interview: built, walls, push out, expand, break down, break the mould, reinforce, lift, break through, scratch, undermine foundations. We are no longer talking about the planning task directly but exploring his metaphors for the planning task.]

SA: I told you about the long-term plan that we do, and we set that up as the start and we come up with a scheme of work for the whole term, the skill and the knowledge that we want the children to have acquired or have experience of through the term. What I'll do then is to take that long-term plan, that sketch plan if you like and look in a more short-term way at a week's activities. Before the weekend, or a week before those activities would start, I sit down and *break that up* into tasks that the children can do. So I'll think of a way . . . So say that for instance I'm doing some work with electricity and I want to introduce the children to simple circuits. One way of doing that would be to sit down and do some chalk and talk on the blackboard and tell them how simple circuits work. But that is not particularly effective with children of that age so I'll think about what I'll send the children to do where they can find out how a simple circuit can work, how they can make a light bulb light up, how a switch works, normally I try and make it as relevant as possible. So it would not just be making a circuit but it would be making a circuit to do something so that it would have a useful purpose.

[A long example was given. This was ignored and the sense (feel) term 'break down' was targeted]

I: So you just talked about breaking tasks down, how is that important?

SA: So I'll look for a common starting point, a starting point where they'll all have access to it. And will be able to succeed at the starting point. I will then think how that particular activity can then be developed, so that the children who are more able and who have the capability can then *pursue the task further*, I'll have that aimed at the various groups according to abilities but I'm very open as to who actually does . . . sometimes within an ability there will be children who just won't be able to get as far as I had anticipated and also there will be children who you had not anticipated being able to do something who will be able to do it so, through watching the children on task you can tell who can be extended on a particular activity and it will vary from task to task.

[There are several sensory terms. Only one is targeted. 'Pursue' is changed to 'expand' by the interviewer. The importance of the task, once more an action being referred to as if it were an object, as something that can be pursued further, is what is followed. Note the details of the sequence of the planning task.]

I: Expanding the task further, how is that important?

SA: It is important in terms of not expecting the same from every child. If I did that I would be doing a disservice to all the children, if I did that then there would be some children who always failed and who would never succeed. And there are some children who would be working well within their capability and would never be *pushing beyond* that. Would never be *extending the boundaries* of what they can do.

I: Extending boundaries, and pushing beyond . . . what? How do you see that? [Exploring the properties of the image. The image is not yet clear but key words are picked on to expand it.]

SA: I see it in two ways. I see it as pushing beyond their own experience. So gaining experience and knowledge beyond what they already acquired. And I also see it in terms of *breaking down* their own limiting perception that they may have of themselves. What they think they can do.

I: Breaking down, what are they breaking down? [Target sensory (feel) term 'breaking down' and exploring the image.]

SA: They are breaking down their limitation, *their walls.* For any given area of the curriculum that wall might be there due to previous experience. If they have been given a task and they've failed miserably at it or they may not have been able to get a successful result, then the next time they come to do something similar already you have a *barrier* that needs overcoming.

I: so in terms of that barrier, that wall you talked about, what do you see your role as being? [Explore how the wall, which is assumed to be the same as the barrier relates to him.]

SA: First of all I have to gauge as well as possible, if the wall the child has set is realistic, have they put it in a place where it is at the limit of their capability, or *is it well in front of that.* There is no point in trying to push them . . .

I: So the wall could be behind them? [Explore the property of location – is there a case where the wall is behind? Predicting what the image contains.]

SA: No, but the wall could be close to them, much closer than it needs to be. [The image is of a child with the wall all around them, so it could not be behind them but can be very close. This leads to a long explanation of his role in breaking the wall down. Deleted.]

I: So *success* means *breaking the wall down.* [A complex equivalence targeted from the previous response. Planning the task to be done by the children well is equivalent to breaking the wall down. As this is suggested the expert agrees emphatically.]

SA: Yes, very much so. I've talked about, part of the process means me being able to gauge where the wall is.

[Section deleted. We move on to talk about the learning process and explore different links between the wall image and learning, the interviewer suggests a path on the basis of language used.]

SA: There will be a limit at any particular moment in time as to *where* they can *get to*.

I: *Get to?* Is it a journey? [Targeting 'get to'. A place where I get to, suggest the possibility of a journey.]

SA: Yes. very much so.

I: So is it a journey? and the IT here is learning? a journey where what you are doing is breaking down different walls that you come across? [Putting together the images produced. Ensuring that we are both talking about the same thing.]

SA: [He now expands on the metaphor explicitly, uses it to explain what the process of learning is like for him] It is almost as if you are on this journey, and it is almost as if you are carrying with you this wall that is around you, so although you may be going along on this journey, the wall will appear in front of you at some point, and it has been put there for various reasons: either by the child himself or by circumstance or by perception they've picked up from other people and that will unnaturally limit them. And it is actually breaking down that built barrier so that they can actually carry on their journey to something that is more like what they can do.

[A long section deleted which explores the [LEARNING IS A JOURNEY]. Notice that we started with a statement without any metaphors. As key words were targeted some isolated images were found; these were explored until the metaphor was produced.]

I: How do you use this understanding of your role and your job, when you are sitting down, at your desk to plan a day? [Searching for more direct links with the planning task.]

SA: If I did not have this view [the metaphor we just explored], then I'd have to interpret what I do with the children in a more limited way, it would probably be in terms of the curriculum that I have to give to the children, that would be my *limitations*. I think that what would happen then is that I would have very specific requirements of the children during the day.

I: So you would be building a wall. [Checking understanding. it was established earlier that a limitation was represented in the image by a wall. This is not used directly in this response.]

SA: I would be building a wall.

[Section deleted. More of the journey metaphor is explored, finding how the different elements of the task fit into it. We move on to discuss tasks.]

SA: Sometimes it's to do with how it's *packaged.* How you present it to the children and you can have a path that is very interesting, that you've not *gift wrapped* at all particularly well, it's like here it is and you hand it to the children and *they can see it straightaway* and it holds no mystique.

I: How do you see that? Is that a present you are giving them? [Explore the properties of the sensory images. Targeting sensory based language and asking how the expert sees the image.]

SA: Yes very much that. Not only if I can *wrap it up* and make it very exciting for them *to unpack* and find out *what is inside,* but it's almost like teasing them with the present and it's something that I will build the anticipation up about. I will perhaps talk about what could possibly be *inside this package,* what could this thing be about? [Expanding on the image.]

I: So the task is the gift? [Checking back that the metaphor we just reached was [A TASK IS A GIFT]]

SA: Yeah and to temporarily hold it back . . . That is much more effective than something that you haven't even taken the price off, you just give it to them.

I: Giving the present unwrapped, would that be the same as providing them with information? [Exploring the consequences of the metaphor and testing where within it the strategy of just providing information, which was mentioned earlier as an unsuccessful strategy, fits.]

SA: Yes very much so. That's absolutely right.

[Section deleted.]

I: Where are the *presents* in the *journey*? [Linking the task with learning. Finding out the links between the two metaphors.]

SA: Well sometimes, they will be carrying the present with them and they'll be taking layer upon layer off as they go along and sometimes you will devise a journey, which seems to be a very simple journey to make and they will come across this parcel lying on their path, they got so far in to the journey then they will want to stop and unwrap what they discovered. Particularly if you can get the child to believe that they have discovered this themselves, it gives them a sense of ownership, they are going to want to do it themselves . . . so you might lead them towards the present rather than give it to them.

[Deleted section. More of the metaphor is explored.]

SA: [The unspecified reference here is to the task] Making sure it has accessibility that it has a starting point where it is easy for them to get started.

I: How does that link with the wall? Is that how you make a hole in the wall? [Linking that back with the image of the wall, checking understanding.]

SA: Yes, if the task is made too difficult to begin with then the wall will still be there and you will have to add more bricks to it, because you've reinforced the perception that they can't do it.

We have presented the interview in this form because it is not obvious how to use interactively the framework in Chapter 5. We could make the mapping of the metaphors to the planning task more explicit, spelling out the structure of the metaphors elicited and how they are linked to the strategic knowledge he uses in planning. We would do this if we wanted to create a model of this knowledge. Our intention here was to give you an extended example of how to use the ideas in Chapters 5 and 6.

Appendix 2: Resources for knowledge management

There is a huge amount of information available on knowledge management. Practise what you have learnt in this book when you make the decision as to what to explore in more depth. There is little available on the personal skills needed for effective knowledge management. We have marked with an asterisk the resources we believe focus most on this aspect of knowledge management.

Books

The following books are a good basis for acquiring an overview of the area, particularly about what it takes from an organizational perspective to create a knowledge-based organization:

Davis, S. and Botkin, J. (1994) *The Monster under the Bed: How Business is Mastering the Opportunity of Knowledge for Profit*. Simon and Schuster.

Opportunities and threats offered by the knowledge revolution are explored. The profound effect that the knowledge paradigm will have on our lives is discussed.

Krantz, S. (1997) *Building Intranets with Lotus Notes & Domino*. Maximum Press. http://www.maxpress.com

Nonaka, I. and Takeuchi, H. (1995) *The Knowledge-Creating Company*. Oxford University Press.

Focuses on the distinction between tacit and explicit knowledge. Japanese business practices to access tacit knowledge are explored.

Skyrme, D. J. and Amidon, D. M. (1997) *Creating the Knowledge Based Business*. Business Intelligence Ltd: Wimbledon.

A comprehensive report on current initiatives. High quality and in-depth. Excellent to gain in-depth knowledge of what organizational initiatives on knowledge management. Good pointers to existing resources such as consultants and software.

Smith C. and Irving P. (1997) *Knowledge Management*. The Institute of Management Foundation. ISBN: 0859462838

Excellent resource of what is available in the area. Short and concise. Contains an abstracts section which summarizes all key literature.

Wiig, K. M. (1993–4) 1. *Knowledge Management Foundations: Thinking about Thinking – How Organisations Create, Represent and Use Knowledge*. 2. *Knowledge Management: The Central Management Focus for Intelligent-Acting Organisations*. 3. *Knowledge Management Methods: Practical Approaches to Managing Knowledge*. Schema Press.

Wikstrom, S. and Normann, R. (1993) *Knowledge and Value: A New Perspective on Corporate Transformation*. Routledge.

Wilson, D. (1996) *Managing Knowledge*. Butterworth-Heinemann.

An organizational perspective on how to exploit organizational knowledge. Explores ways to use knowledge for predicting future trends.

The following books, though not all aimed at the business world, are particularly good to gain greater depth in the further development of your knowledge skills:

Diaper, D. (ed.) (1988) *Knowledge Elicitation: Principles, Techniques and Applications*. Ellis Horwood.

Hussey, J. and Hussey, R. (1997) *Business Research: A Practical Guide for Undergraduate and Postgraduate Students*. MacMillan Business.

Leonard-Barton, D. (1995) *Wellsprings of Knowledge: Building and Sustaining the Sources of Innovation*. Harvard Business School Press.

McGraw, K. L. and Harbison-Briggs, K. (1989) *Knowledge Acquisition: Principles and Guidelines*. Prentice-Hall.

Tobin, D. R. (1996) *Transformational Learning: Renewing your Company through Knowledge and Skills*. John Wiley.

Articles

David, S. and Botkin, J. (1994) The coming of the knowledge-based business. *Harvard Business Review*, September–October, 165–170.

Houlder, V. (1996) The power of knowledge. *Financial Times*, 1 September, 14.

van Krogh, G. and Roos, J. (1996) Five claims on knowing. *European Management Journal*, **14** (4), August, 423–426.

Leighton, P. (1996) Gardeners' question time. *Human Resources UK*, (26), September–October, 94–95, 97.

Lloyd, B. (1996) Knowledge management: the key to long term organisational success. *Long Range Planning*, **29** (40), August, 576–580.

Mullin, R. (1996) Knowledge management: a cultural evolution. *Journal of Business Strategy*, **17** (5), September–October, 56–59.

Murray, P. and Myers, A. (1997) The facts about knowledge. *Information Strategy*, **2** (7), September.

Nonaka, I. (1991) The knowledge creating company. *Harvard Business Review*, **69** (6), November–December, 96–104.

Quinn, J. B., Anderson, P. and Finkelstein, S. (1996) Leveraging intellect. *Academy of Management Executive*, **10** (3), November, 7–27.

Sveiby, K. (1993) The know-how company. *International Journal of Strategic Management*, **3**, John Wiley.

van de Vliet, A. (1997) Lest we forget. *Management Today*, January, 62–64.

Journals

Knowledge Management. Ark Publishing London. ark@dircon.co.uk

Knowledge and Process Management. Tel: 01865 791100

Journal of Knowledge Management. Tel: 01243 854499

Web sites

Some sites which may be of interest in finding out what is available. Where the addresses are not self-explanatory, we have added the full name of the organization the site belongs to next to the address in bold. These are not part of the address.

http://kmn.cibit.hvu.nl **The Knowledge Management Network**

http://www.3-cities.com/home/bonewman/public_htm1/ index.html **Knowledge Management Forum**

http://www.brint.com/

http://www.idongroup.co./magnet/magnet.htm#magbottom **Suppliers of Hexagons**

http://www.knowledge.stjohns.co.uk/ **Knowledge Associates International**

http://www.nijenrode.nl/games/metaplan.html **Suppliers of Metaplan**

http://www.sun.com **Lotus Development Corp and Sun Microsystems**

www.domino. lotus.com

www.info-strategy.com **Information Strategy Magazine**

www.lotus.com

www.microsoft.com

Consultants

We have only included phone numbers for contacting consultancy firms. Complete details are widely available from many sources. KSD is the consultancy firm owned by the authors. It runs workshops and consultancy projects specializing in the development of knowledge skills in an organizational context.

Arthur Andersen Consulting: + 44 171 438 3158
Contact: Terry Finerty

ASLIB (The Association for Information Management)
Tel: 0171 253 4488

Courtney Consulting: 0181 693 8971

ENTOVATION International: 01635 551434

Ernst and Young: + 44 171 931 5029
Contact: Philip Fearnley

KSD (Knowledge Skills Development) Associates:
+44 181 944 0116

Price Waterhouse: +44 171 939 6487
Contact: Jon Z. Bentley

Renaissance Solutions: 0171 290 3700

Research and development

The Cranfield School of Management: carry out research under the heading 'European Knowledge Management Project'. Contact: Andrew Myers and Peter Murray.

Lotus Development Corporation: a subsidiary of IBM. Lotus Services Group provides consulting, support and educational services.

Roffey Park Management Institute: has carried out research on knowledge transfer skills in professional developers. Contact: Mariana Funes.

The above are some highlights to point you towards some of the resources available on related topics not directly covered in this book. The Bibliography provides you with an extensive resource list, should you want to pursue in depth any of the topics we have presented in the previous pages. Happy knowledge capturing!

Appendix 3: Some knowledge terms*

Artificial intelligence. The study of computational techniques for symbol manipulation where the structures have an intended interpretation that is expressive of knowledge or other things relevant to our understanding of human intelligence or the understanding of behaviour that we recognize as intelligent.

Compiled knowledge. In the case where knowledge is expressed such that the reasons why it holds together are not also expressed, the knowledge is said to be compiled.

Concept. A concept is an abstraction we make on people's ability to make judgements. We can say of persons who can add up, divide, etc. that they have the 'concept' of number. In this way of speaking, to have a concept is to have a certain ability to make judgements. It is harmless to talk directly of a concept, instead of the ability to make the judgements that constitute having the concept. In this usage, a concept can be thought of as an object that conveys the requisite information and inferences typically associated with judgement.

*Based on Mital and Johnson, 1992

Conceptual analysis. Analysing the judgements made in a given domain. The analysis reveals a cluster of interrelated CONCEPTS.

Expert. One who has organized and COMPILED KNOWLEDGE in such a way as to be above averagely effective and efficient at a particular task or set of tasks.

Expert system. A piece of software encoding knowledge. The knowledge is domain specific and there are experts. The systems should give an EXPLANATION of its behaviour from a reconstruction of its INFERENCE paths. The system should perform at the level of the EXPERT, and should do so in a way that is responsive to the user's needs. Not every system so called has all these characteristics.

Explanation. An account of why certain things are the way they are. An explanation could have certain pragmatic features like reducing the unfamiliar to the familiar and are given in answer to questions such as How? or Why?

Heuristic. A device, trick or rule of thumb which is the basis of an INFERENCE where the conclusion is not clear.

Hierarchy. A structure in which some of the elements are subordinate to others. A strict hierarchy is graphically shown as an inverted tree with a single root element at the top. A tangled hierarchy has elements with more than one superordinate element.

Inference. Assertion made on the basis of something else. Inference chains are used to represent reasoning.

Information system. A computer system whose basic purpose is to represent/store, transform or manipulate data.

Knowledge acquisition. The processes aimed at encapsulating some pertinent knowledge for a knowledge or EXPERT system. It usually calls for knowledge elicitation, that is, the identification of the sources, the drawing from the sources and the analysis of the data so collected in order to determine some of what is known by the EXPERTS and related personnel.

Knowledge engineer. A specialist in KNOWLEDGE ACQUISITION.

Life cycle. The individual phases and functions of a software development sequence considered as an integral, continuous process. As such the life cycle is to be managed.

Meta-knowledge. The structures, if any, which encode how the represented knowledge operates or is organized.

Procedure. The sequence of actions.

Prototype. A version of the system deliberately designed to do less that the final system is envisaged to do and designed or built specifically for evaluation. The prototype does not a have all the functionality or reliability of the final system.

Strategic knowledge. The knowledge of how to select a subTASK on the basis of the data at hand.

Task tree. A breakdown of a TASK into a HIERARCHY of subTASKS.

Task. The thing to be done.

Appendix 4:
More knowledge IT*

This appendix goes into greater detail on the different software packages, technologies and approaches to support knowledge management.

Net technologies

The same technical standards underlie all net technologies.

- Internet – connects everyone.
- Intranets – connect individuals within a company.
- Extranets – connect companies to one another.
- Groupware: Lotus Notes Groupware, Screen Cams – supports virtual teams/organizations.

Knowledge-based systems

- Artificial intelligence, e.g. neural networks, expert systems and intelligent networks.

*Our thanks to Valerie Garrow

- Case-based reasoning, i.e., uses a reasoning process to solve problems which are similar to others which have already been solved.
- Information systems that model the workings of an organism.

Data storage

- Data mining.
- Data warehouses – (probably where companies can rent space on a more powerful system).

Knowledge management architectures (KMAs)

Assessment tools

KMAT

Knowledge Management Assessment Tool (Arthur Andersen and American Productivity and Quality Center [APQC]), 1995). A diagnostic tool to benchmark KM processes. Also includes an Organization Knowledge Management Model (OKMM) covering twenty-four knowledge management practices under the headings: leadership, technology, culture, measurement and process. This can be used for external or internal benchmarking. (There is a charge for benchmarking against an external company.)

Measures of intellectual capital

The Skandia Navigator

Similarities with the Balanced Scorecard, i.e., measures in several dimensions including financial, customer human, process, renewal. Skandia describe it as a 'taxonomy of intellectual capital reporting'. It is essentially a model of measures which balances human and structural capital – putting intellectual assets on the balance sheet or annual report (goodwill in a merger/takeover).

Dow Chemical: IAM (Intellectual Asset Model)

Four levels of comprehensive measurement should cover: corporate, global business, functional and individual.

Collaborative technologies

CompuServe

A public on-line service which can be used to develop a network infrastructure to provide access from world-wide locations. Includes electronic mail, private on-line forums, virtual conferencing.

Lotus Notes

Lotus Notes is a document database which offers different views of databases, e.g. by process, industry, company, topic, performance measure. It can be thought of as envelopes which take a variety of items and assists in workflow and automated business processes. Its great advantage is the ability to replicate so that remote stations can work on and change a document, sharing knowledge and using brainstorming techniques. Its search facility is also a powerful tool, e.g. for providing a complete customer profile from existing knowledge. It resembles Windows Programme Manager and contains applications such as databases, discussion threads. There is also a NotesBench Consortium Web site run by an independent organization dedicated to providing Domino and Notes performance information to customers. There are 10 million Notes users world-wide. Other software systems can be built on top of Lotus Notes, e.g. 'Knowledge Express' of American Management Systems.

Lotus Domino (powered by Lotus Notes)

The first groupware and e-mail server for the Net. Lotus Domino is an applications and messaging server with an integrated set of services. Notes and Domino offer calendaring and scheduling features, directory services and replication:

- *Lotus Domino Mail Server* enables the deployment of messaging, integrated calendaring and scheduling, news groups, discussions and Web access. Interoperates with other mail systems.

- *Lotus Learning Space* – distributed learning technology delivers training and education to geographically dispersed students (cf. also First Class used by the Open University).

Microsoft Commercial Internet System (MCIS, codenamed Normandy)

Designed for conducting business on-line but dependent on third party applications for many functions. It is a set of servers governing the primary Internet functions, e.g. mail, news, data replication and searching.

Microsoft Outlook

A desktop information management program which enables people to organize and share information, communicate with others, manage messages, appointments, contacts and tasks, track activities. Information is organized in folders. There is an Inbox to read and send mail and requests. E-mail names and Internet addresses are converted automatically to live hyperlinks and a Document Map facility organizes e-mail messages quickly. Word detects if a message contains a long conversation thread and creates a map, via hyperlinks, to each message. It can be used as a substitute to Windows Explorer.

Microsoft NetMeeting

Uses the Internet to deliver audio and video conferencing to desktop machines where users can share whiteboard data, files, applications and text chat.. Can be downloaded free from the Microsoft Web site (www.microsoft.com/msdownload/netmeeting2).

Combined technology

Sun Microsystems and the Lotus Development Corp have combined hardware, software and service solutions to provide messaging and Internet solutions which can be used as a platform for deploying Internet, intranet and extranet applications.

Intranet

Intranet is an internal company network built using Internet technology. Multimedia facilities linked to relevant people and information, e.g. ICL's Café VIK set up as a web site on ICL's intranet with a friendly design using a cartoon character. Business benefits identified by ICL are being able to contact client managers quickly, greater awareness of customer issues and opportunities, specialists can access 'technology watch' for latest briefings.

An example of two knowledge sharing and creating systems in Arthur Andersen:

Convergent systems	*Divergent systems*
● Codified information	● Not extensively codified
● Top down	● Bottom up
● All information verified	● Not all verified
● Periodically updated	● Real-time input/debate
● Historical information	● Innovative/work in progress
● Disseminating	● Creating
● Classification	● Fluid categories
● Not group centric	● Group centric
● Information extracted from field	● Information offered by field

Cross-industry work groups

For example, GlaxoWellcome, Ford, GM, Xerox, Kraft, Coca Cola, and the US army are all members of two cross-industry work groups facilitated by APQC and Boston University.

Databases (examples)

- Experiences database (Yellow Pages) – skills and experience of all staff.
- Company information.
- Product and service innovations.
- Opportunity – insider information on prospects.

Business intelligence

Converting information by expert filtering, editing, archiving and researching, i.e. information that has been processed into a more useful format.

Examples of products

Knowledger (Knowledge Associates Product) uses World Wide Web and/or Lotus Notes:

1 *Personal Development Plan (PDP)* – part of 'Knowledger' an integrated suite of Lotus Notes applications – strategic software technology. This is a 'living document' used to maximize competence and career development. Users can match their experiences with competencies. It provides an updated skills database and reports on individual and organizational learning. Aid to structuring PD and ensures maximum benefit from training. Also links in with Investors in People and supports competence system.

2 *Personal Knowledge Manager (PKM)* – (part of Knowledger turns personal information into shared knowledge) enables individuals, teams and organizations to develop, share and retain knowledge, values, vision and principles. *Lotus InterNotes* – Internet and intranet through automatic and distributed Web Publishing. Increases communication, collaboration

3 *Knowledge Accounting System* – measures and compares human knowledge capital (rates, levels, types of learning, strategic and core competency levels), structural capital (better business process performance ratios, shared best practices and knowledge base 'hits', and customer capital (retention and loyalty ratios). E-mail for information: info.knowledge@stjohns.co.uk

Meltingpoint (Docuwork)

Notes:

1 Meltingpoint builds a company specific model of patterns of data and information usage. Documents, data objects, users comments – everything is related to every relevant other.

2 Meltingpoint's uniqueness stems from allowing information from any application to be linked to information in any other. Similarly, discussions, comments etc. can be cross-referenced (even as links to an HTML interface). The effect is that different systems, e.g. legacy, client server and desktop, work together as one. No matter how complex the links the user is presented only with

what is relevant in context. It does this without changing user interfaces, security or functionality, querying or form filling.

3 Meltingpoint scans growing knowledge and alerts the user in real time to relevant information and links made by work colleagues.

4 Meltingpoint does all this by managing relationships that already exist inside the data. It is not an artificial intelligence system where you must explicitly represent the knowledge in a knowledge base. It is a knowledge management tool on a commercial scale.

Company examples of knowledge technology

Allied Domecq

- Competitive databases.
- Project tracking system.
- Project development database.
- EIS for tracking movements towards destination.
- MIS for looking at knowledge and information.
- Consumer research.

Dow

Intellectual asset management (IAM) Global Technology Centre responsible for:

- continuous IAM process improvement
- identifying and communicating best technology
- database management
- measurement – integrated set of measures at four levels – corporate, business area, functional and individual
- developing core competencies
- cross-industry benchmarking
- 28,000 computers connected to corporate computer network
- intranet and World Wide Web
- key pieces of know-how on one-page fact sheets stored on database with key contacts, references and relation to other areas of business.

Glaxo

Core network resources:

- client browser access
- security system inbuild
- directory service (Yellow Pages project)
- search/index for search and cataloguing
- thesaurus – helps retrieval
- publishing – ability to publish on Intranet
- data-mining and analysis facility.

British Airways

British Airways uses Lotus Notes for a variety of learning and change processes. The Change Forum is an application allowing requests for changes, e.g. putting on a larger aircraft for a particularly heavy load. All requests are posted and every stakeholder (e.g. marketing, scheduling, crewing, etc.) in the process is able to see the stage the request is at. Each party is able to comment on difficulties and accept or reject the request. Once all parties have given the go ahead the change is made. As it is now an easier process rather than the previous tedious method of sending telexes, more changes are made with increased profits.

The Mods Forum is another application with a built in e-mail so that responses can be prompted. It is used for technical adjustments to aircraft and has a built in analysis function which calculates cost and work involved. Pilots' flight reports can be accessed and used as a learning tool where similar incidents have happened before rather than filed.

British Petroleum (BP)

With over thirty key partners and suppliers BP shares desktop collaboration, video conferencing and information tools (Virtual Teamwork Programme). An electronic Yellow Pages lists people by interest, expertise and experience. To support this coaching is provided in collaborative working and BP is building up a showcase of KM case studies.

After Action Reviews (AARs) – designed in US army and used by Motorola and General Electric – a mechanism to capture learning from four questions:

- What was supposed to happen?
- What actually happened?
- Why were there differences?
- What can we learn?

Buckman Laboratories

Developed K'Netix – an intranet which connects all employees, particularly associates who were working in different parts of the world, to knowledge resources and contacts. The driving force was to increase customer contact and a Vice-President of Knowledge Transfer was appointed in 1991. K'Netix allows access to experts and library resources, problem-solving groups, unrestricted communication across geographical locations. Benefits include speed of response to customers, improved creativity of new products.

Price Waterhouse (Knowledge View – implemented in Lotus Notes)

'A repository of knowledge and information.' This is a framework for sharing knowledge and integrating knowledge from different parts of the business.

It contains ten databases with over 20,000 documents the main one of which is KIT (Knowledge and Information Transfer). The latter contains best practice information, internal and external benchmarking studies, expert opinions including own knowledge, client experience and research, abstracts of books and articles about methods and tools, trends and issues, views and forecasts of Price Waterhouse's experts, other sources and practitioners. Information is held in a common format: Change Drivers, Practice Before, Practice After, Benefits/Performance Measures, Lessons Learned, Where to Next.

Price Waterhouse has a common descriptive language to describe business processes: The International Business Language (a registered service mark). This enables users to find equivalent processes across industries and, for example, find examples of situations which have had the same change drivers but different outcomes.

Bibliography

Bandler, R. and Grinder, J. (1975) *The Structure of Magic*. Vols 1 and 2, Science and Behavior Books.

Bandler, R. and Grinder, J. (1979) *Frogs into Princes*. Real People Press.

Bandler, R. and Macdonald, W. (1988) *An Insider's Guide to Submodalities*. Meta Publications.

Bateson, G. (1972) *Steps to an Ecology of Mind*. Chandler Publishing Company.

Bateson, M.C. (1989) *Composing a Life*. Penguin.

Bateson, M.C. (1994) *Peripheral Visions: Learning along the Way*. HarperCollins.

Bateson, M.C. (1997) NLP Comprehensive International Conference, 'Intuition – Making Sense of a Complex World'.

Bretto, C. (1990) *A Framework for Excellence: A Resource Manual for NLP.* Centre for Professional Development, Santa Cruz, Ca. USA.

Buzan, T. and Buzan, B. (1993) *The Mind Map Book*. BBC Books.

Chervet, S.R. (1995) *Words that Change Minds: Mastering the Language of Influence*. Kendall/Hunt Publishing.

Claxton, G. (1996) Structure, strategy and self. *Journal of Consciousness Studies*, 3 (2).

Claxton, G. (1997) *Hare Brain and Tortoise Mind*. Fourth Estate.

Clegg, B. (1998) *The Chameleon Manager*. Butterworth-Heinemann.

Clegg, B. and Birch, P. (1998) *DisOrganization*. Pitman.

Collins, H., Green, R. H. and Draper, R. C. (1985) Where's the expertise? In *Expert Systems 85 : Proceedings of the Fifth*

Technical Conference of the British Computer Society (M. Merry, ed.), Cambridge.

Csikszentmihalyi, M. (1996) *The Psychology of Optimal Experience.* Harper & Row.

Csikszentmihalyi, M. (1997) *Finding Flow: The Psychology of Engagement of Everyday Life.* HarperCollins.

De Bono, E. (1990) *I Am Right And You Are Wrong.* Penguin Books.

Denzin, N.K. (1978b) *The Research Act.* McGraw Hill.

Dilts, R., Grinder, J., Bandler, R. and DeLozier, J. (1980) *Neuro-Linguistic Programming: The Study of Subjective Experience.* Meta Publications.

Dreyfus, H. (1992) *What Computers Still Can't Do: A Critique of Artificial Reason.* MIT press.

Dreyfus, H. and Dreyfus, S. (1989) *Mind over Machine: The Power of Human Intuition and Expertise in the Era of the Computer.* Blackwell.

Feigenbaum, E., McCorduck, P. and Nii, H. P (1988) *The Rise of the Expert Company: How Visionary Companies are Using Artificial Intelligence to Achieve Higher Productivity and Profits.* Macmillan.

Funes, M. (1995) *Structuring Metaphors as Understanding*, Rapport.

Funes, M. (1997) *Plerking Around.* Management Training and Skills.

Funes M. (1998 forthcoming) A cognitive model for knowledge transfer: What has bridging got to do with development? *Roffey Park Management Institute Research Report.*

Geus, A. de (1997) *The Living Company.* Nicholas Brealey.

Ghazi, P. and Jones, J. (1997) *Getting a Life.* Hodder and Stoughton.

Glynn, C. (1996) *Unlocking the Secrets of the Long-lived.* Roffey Park Report, Roffey Park Management Institute.

Goleman, D. (1995) *Emotional Intelligence.* Bloomsbury Publishing.

Goodheart, A. (1994) *Laughter Therapy.* Less Stress Press.

Graunke, B. and Roberts, T. (1985) Neurolinguistic programming: The impact of imagery task on sensory predicate usage. *Journal of Counselling Psychology,* **32** (4), 525–530.

Gumm, W., Walker, M. and Day, H. (1982) Neuro linguistic programming: Method or myth? *Journal of Counselling Psychology,* **29** (3), 327–330.

Heggie, J. (1994) Body–mind phrases. *Anchor Point,* **8** (5), 30–34, Cahill Mountain Press.

Heron J. (1996) *Co-operative Inquiry: Research into the Human Condition.* Sage.

Holbeche, L. (1994) *Career Development in Flatter Structures.* Roffey Park Management Institute.

Horner, J. (1996) If the eye were an animal . . . . *Journal of Consciousness Studies*, **3**, (2).

Howard, J. (1998) *Managing More With Less*. Butterworth-Heinemann.

IIR Ltd (1997) *Overcoming the cultural barriers and building practical frameworks for effective knowledge management*, conference proceedings, 28–30 January, London.

Information Strategy (1997) **2** (7), The Economist Group.

James, T. and Woodsmall, W. (1988) *Time Line Therapy and the Basis of Personality*. Meta Publications.

Johnson, L., Johnson N. E. and Funes, M. (1998) Knowledge management: the role of knowledge skills. Paper in preparation.

Johnson, M. (1981) *Philosophical Perspectives on Metaphor*. University of Minnesota Press.

Koestler, A. (1964) *The Act of Creation*. Macmillan.

Kolb, D. (1985) *Experiential Learning: Experience as the Source of Learning and Development*. Prentice-Hall.

Laborde, G. Z. (1988) *Fine Tune Your Brain: When Everything's Going Right and What to Do When It Isn't . . . .* Syntony Publishing.

Lakoff, G. (1987) Cognitive models and prototype theory. In *Concepts and Conceptual Development* (U. Neisser, ed.), Cambridge University Press.

Lakoff, G. and Johnson, M. (1980a) *Metaphors We Live By*. University of Chicago Press.

Lakoff, G. and Johnson, M. (1980b) The metaphorical structure of the conceptual system. *Cognitive Science*, **4**, 195–208.

Leonard, D. (1997) Mining knowledge assets for innovation. *Knowledge Management*, **1** (1).

Mayo, E. (1997) *New Economics Magazine*. Issue 40. New Economics Foundation.

Mellon, L. (1996) A case of do-it-yourself. *The Guardian*, 19 October.

Mital, V. and Johnson, L. (1992) *Advanced Information Systems for Lawyers*. Chapman and Hall.

Morik, K. (1991) Underlying assumptions of knowledge acquisition and machine learning. *Knowledge Acquisition*, **3**, 137–156.

Musen, M. (1988) Conceptual Models of Interactive Knowledge Acquisition Tools. Second European workshop in knowledge acquisition for knowledge based systems. 26 June, Bonn.

Newell, A. and Simon, H. (1972) Computer science as empirical enquiry: symbols and search. In *Mind Design*, (J. Hangeland ed), Bradford Books.

Nonaka, I. (1991) The knowledge creating company. *Harvard Business Review*, **69** (6).

Palmer J. (1997) The Human Organisation. Amed Research and Development Conference, August.

Patton, M. W. (1990) *Qualitative Evaluation and Research Methods*. Sage.

Polanyi, M. (1958) *Personal Knowledge*. Routledge and Kegan Paul.

Rechtschaffen, S. (1996) *Timeshifting*. Rider Books.

Salas, J., Degroot, H. and Spanos, N. (1989) NLP and hypnotic responding: an empirical evaluation. *Journal of Mental Imagery,* **13** (1), 79–90.

Schon, D. (1988) From technical rationality to reflection in action. In *Professional Judgement: A Reader in Clinical Decision Making,* (J. Dowie and A. Elstein, eds), Cambridge University Press.

Semler, R. (1993) *Maverick*. Warner Books.

Shapiro E. C. (1995) *Fad Surfing in the Boardroom: Reclaiming the Courage to Manage in the Age of Instant Answers*. Addison Wesley.

Shepard, R. and Metzler, J. (1971) Mental Rotation of 3D objects. *Science*, February, 701–703.

Sperber, D. and Wilson, D. (1986) *Relevance: Communication and Cognition*. Blackwell.

Spradley, J. P. (1979) *The Ethnographic Interview*. Holt Reinhart and Winston.

Spretnak C. (1993) *States of Grace: The Recovery of Meaning in the Postmodern Age*. HarperCollins.

Sveiby, K. (1993) The know how company. *International Journal of Strategic Management,* **3**, John Wiley.

Sweetser, E. (1987) Metaphorical models of thought and speech. *Proceedings of the 13th Annual Meeting of the Berkeley Linguisitcs Society.*

Sweetser, E. (1990) *From Etymology to Pragmatics: Metaphorical and Cultural Aspects of Semantic Structure*. Cambridge University Press.

Wofford, J. C (1994) Getting inside the leader's head: a cognitive processes approach to leadership. *SAM Advanced Management Journal*, Summer.

Woodward, B. (1988) Knowledge Acquisition at the Front End: Defining the Domain. Third Knowledge Acquisition for Knowledge Based Systems Workshop, Banff, Canada.

Wurman, R. S. (1989) *Information Anxiety*. Pan Books.

Yeager, J. (1985) *Thinking about Thinking with NLP*. Meta Publications.

Index